Trav

by

Marianne Hulse

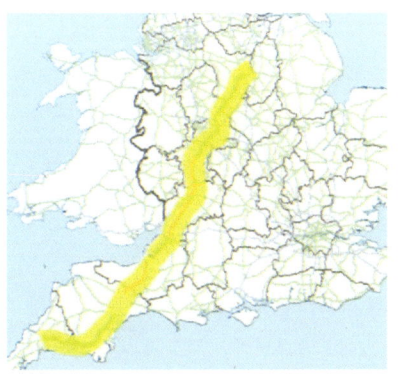

Contents

The Writer 4
The Driver 4
Day 0 6
Day 1 9
Day 2 19
Day 3 26
Day 4 33
Day 5 39
Day 6 46
Day 7 54
Day 8 59
Day 9 65
Day 10 71
Day 11 76
Day 12 85
Day 13 95
Day 14 105
Day 15 112
Day 16 120
Where did we go? 127
Some costs 129
Postscript 133

The Writer
and a swan in Exeter

The Driver
resting on Dartmoor

We had both travelled thousands of miles around Britain while we were working. The road we saw sign-posted the most was the A38. It seemed to be everywhere.

One day I said to the driver, "Is that our A38?"
"Yes," he said. "It's a very long road."

So we looked it up and found that it starts in Mansfield, goes past our back door, and ends up in Cornwall. It is about 290 miles long, and is the second longest A Road in Britain (The longest is the A1 which goes from London to Edinburgh).

Well, we were interested, the A38 runs close to our home in Derbyshire, and the idea of exploring the road took hold.

We booked some leave, did some research, stopped the milk and set off.

We travelled down the M5 and the A30 to Cornwall. The journey to Bodmin took seven hours.

It took 16 days to come back.

Day 0

Friday 11th May 2007

We set off from Belper in Derbyshire at **12:36**. We have exact times for this journey because we synchronised our Sat-Navs as we set off. It seemed important to know exactly how long the journey south would take, because we were going to spend a long time on the return journey. I have a Garmin, the driver has a Tom-Tom, and we compared the expected time of arrival on both Sat-Navs. They were in agreement.

On the way we listened to Terry Wogan's 'Janet and John' stories from a CD that a friend had given us. I hoped that the driver wasn't identifying too closely with John. Poor John.

At **13:32** we stopped at **Strensham Services** on the M5 in Worcester and watched sparrows bathing in the fountains.

The driver had bacon, sausage, fried bread, tomato and mushrooms for lunch. I decided on scrambled egg on toast, which was a mistake. It wasn't very good. Never mind, onwards. We bought some petrol and left the services at **15:01**.

At **15:46** we were halfway between home and the Westbury Hotel in Bodmin according to the Sat Navs.

16:02 Very heavy rain
16:31 Passing the Wellington Monument, very, very heavy rain.

16:34 Reached Devon
16:53 Exeter Services. Had a loo break and bought some maps.
17:11 Left the services – Heavy rain.

17:30 Going around Dartmoor on the A30 – very sunny, clear blue skies over Dartmoor.

17:40 Left the edge of Dartmoor- heavy cloud.

"Does Dartmoor have its own weather system?" I asked the driver.
"It might have," he said.

17:51 Reached Cornwall.
18:04 Passed the **Jamaica Inn**.

This was exciting. Although it wasn't part of <u>the trip</u> we decided to go back and have a look.

Jamaica Inn is the actual building where Daphne du Maurier based her book of the same name. It is supposed to have been used by smugglers and is also supposed to be haunted.

We went in and had dinner at a table close to the brass plaque on the floor which tells you that this is where Joss Merlyn was murdered. The driver had sausages and I had steak and kidney pudding.

"Do you think we will see his ghost?" I asked.
"He's not having any of my sausages," the driver said, "I think he was a fictional character anyway."

It was all very good, including the Jamaica Inn Ale.

19:21 Left the Jamaica Inn.
19:35 Arrived at the **Westbury Hotel**, Bodmin

We had decided that we would only pre-book places to stay at weekends and we would find somewhere on our travels the rest of the time. After all, we could always drive home if things went awry. I had chosen the Westbury Hotel on the internet. It was a good starting point for our expedition.

The driver is a keen musician, and likes to play guitar and sing whenever he has the opportunity. Bodmin Folk Club was putting on a concert at the **Barley Sheaf** that evening.

After a cup of tea at the hotel we walked to the Barley Sheaf. The concert was great; the main guest was Jeff Warner, an American singer and collector of songs.

The driver performed a few songs in the second half, and we drank Tribute Premium Cornish Ale. This ale was brewed at the St Austell Brewery and was created to commemorate the solar eclipse in 1999. It was very good.

(The Bodmin Folk club no longer meets at the Barley Sheaf, you should look at their website for their current location.)

On the way back to the hotel we had a look round the **Hole in the Wall** pub which looked an interesting place to drink.

It was once a debtors' prison and you go through a gated courtyard to get to the pub area. We were too late, it was just closing, but next time we are in Bodmin it will definitely be on our list.

"Good beginning," said the driver.
"Very good beginning," I said. "Tomorrow we start the journey back."

Day 1

Saturday 12th May 2007

The hotel bed was very bouncy and the driver stole the quilt in the night. Some discussion took place about whether we should book twin beds in future.

The bathroom had a mirror with lights around it. We called it the 'star mirror' because it made you feel like a film star. We took photographs of all the rooms and bathrooms during our trip. We have made a slide show of the bathrooms. Does this make us a bit sad?

The room was fine, although the hotel had provided cups, not mugs. We prefer a mug of coffee in the morning (but that's just us). The breakfast was very good.
Driver: Grapefruit and full English.
Me: Strawberries, kiwi and melon, scrambled eggs, fried bread, tomato and mushrooms.
We both had toast and coffee.

The butter was yellow, and served in a round white dish. It looked just like half a boiled egg. We like butter in a dish, rather than in foil packets.

Outside it was raining. You could see the Hole in the Wall pub from the Westbury restaurant (through the heavy rain).

We walked around the charity shops in Bodmin looking for mugs to use in hotel rooms where mugs are not provided. Having looked at all the charity shops I bought two melamine mugs from Millets.

We also bought some plastic folders from WH Smiths and some postcards. We planned to send postcards to my son and his wife, Jim and Rosie, every day of the trip. They were living in a remote house in Wales, up a long steep track. I did wonder if the person delivering the cards every day would also appreciate the daily update.

We wrote the postcards, posted them and packed up the car.

"Are you ready?" I asked the driver.
"Let's start back," he said.
We went to look for the start of the Road.

At **10:30** we thought we had found the start of the A38 (Cooksland Road). The driver got out of the car to take some photographs.

Is this the start?

10:41 Having driven a short way, and been confused by signs, maps and our two Sat-Navs we realised that we were not sure where the A38 actually started. There was a small argument between myself and the driver as to where **the Road** starts.

We went back up Cooksland Road, Launceston Road and back to the A30.

Is this the start?

Well, we set off from here, having decided that it might be. And after all, in the overall journey, does it really matter?

I did some research on the A38 before we set off and found that there is an organisation for people who are interested in roads. This is SABRE, The Society for All British and Irish Road Enthusiasts. They have heaps of information about the A38 and I later looked up details of the start.

They explain that there are two junctions with the A30 near Bodmin.

One is north of the town, and then the road heads off southwards (this is really the start).

Then the road goes round the town and meets the A30 again.

That probably explains our confusion – two junctions with the A30

Our plan now was that the only A road we would travel on would be the A38, and we would drive all of the A38, even looping back if we though a bypass might have been added. Apart from that we were going to explore!

Our first stop was to take a picture of a bridge over the River Fowey.

At this stage we took pictures of everything.

We would be following the Fowey as well as the A38 for a few miles. The river, the A38 and the railway line run through the Glynn Valley. The railway line runs over eight impressive stone viaducts in the valley.

Another time we would really like to come back and take a kayak out on the river, as parts of it are navigable. It starts on Bodmin Moor and runs to the harbour and estuary at Fowey.

We drove under the viaduct near this bridge and took some photographs of the woods. The hedgerows and trees were all green with the lushness of May. Bluebells and pink campions were everywhere in the road banks, life was good, and we were on holiday.

Following the A38, the next place we found was **Largin Wood**. We stopped the car, opened our umbrellas and went for a walk in the woods.

The woods were lovely, full of nesting birds and flowers. One of the Cornwall Railway viaducts could be seen from the woods. Inside the wood you can see the rise of **Largin Castle** which is a camp or fort from the Iron Age.

We were in need of tea and a comfort break after our walk and we found **Trago Mills**, **Liskeard** which looked an interesting place to stop. The car park for the Trago Mills shopping area has a really stunning view of another of the Cornish Railway viaducts.

We had a cup of tea in the 'Keg and Kettle' lakeside restaurant, looked at the birds, and at the water wheel.

In the next picture I am looking down at the water wheel. Note the umbrella!

Next we drove to **Two Waters Foot**, just because we liked the name. We had thought to walk there, but it was raining very heavily, so we decided to drive the small roads around the area instead. This was the reason that we happened on the **Carnglaze Caverns**.

There are tours through the caverns but it was a little while before the next tour would start, so we went for a walk round the woods. They were full of azealas and aquilegias in glorious bloom, and fairy houses. You can buy fairies in the shop, and the driver bought one for his daughter (You may not believe in fairies but we have seen where they live).

The cavern tour was well worth the wait. They were setting up for a concert taking place that evening in the first cavern, apparently the acoustics are tremendous.

As well as the stage, there is a collection of minerals in the first cavern. The second cavern gives you some flavour of what it was like to work in a slate mine. The third cavern has a lake - stunning water, very clear and turquoise coloured and apparently it is potable.

"What does potable mean?" I asked the driver.
"You can drink it," he said.

The guide was friendly and interesting, as were all the people running the caverns.

I believe that you can get married there now. I think this would be great, but I would recommend woolly dresses, as the temperature is a constant 10 degrees. But you would be out of the rain.

Both the driver and I thoroughly enjoyed the caverns, the woods and the gift shop. I don't think they are open on Sundays, so just as well we were there on Saturday.

Next we drove along the future A38 construction works – well, it was future construction when we were there in May 2007.

We have since driven along the Dobwalls bypass through the Glynn Valley. It was opened in the winter of 2008.

Next stop was **Menheniot Station** where we took a picture of **the Car**.

We used the Information point at the station (because it was there) and waved to the train as it passed.

We both like trains. We have a shared sense of excitement about watching trains. Why is it that you feel compelled to say, "Look, a train!" to your companions when you see one? When I was young my mother used to take our family on expeditions to watch the trains. We children used to stand on the railway bridge and watch as the steam trail went beneath us.

We were looking for the pond near Menheniot station, it was shown on the map, but we couldn't find a way to it. I have looked it up on Google Earth, it is clearly shown and is probably a flooded quarry.

The rain had stopped. Next we headed for the coast on the other side of the A38.

We drove past **Castle Air** and the driver took a picture of the plane in their car park. The driver is interested in planes, having had flying lessons in his youth.

Castle Air is a company which sells and charters helicopters and also supplies them for television and film use.

We were following the course of the **River Seaton**.

We parked and walked along the river for a while and took some photographs. I took some action photos of the driver taking photos of the river. I was very disappointed to find that they were all out of focus.

The Seaton is another river which starts on Bodmin Moor. It flows through Hessenford and comes out on the beach at Seaton.

The driver then decided that we needed petrol so we doubled back to the A38 and went to the Shell service station at **Trerulefoot**.

This was close by the **Route 38** Coffee bar and American diner.

We didn't go in this time, but have had an excellent dinner there on a different journey.

Blue skies! We drove back to the River Seaton and through **Hessenford** where there are several B&Bs, including the pub, and some attractive walks along the river. We plan to go back there another time and stay in the village for a few days.

We arrived on the coast at **Seaton**, put on our wellies and walked down the river to the sea.

We were very taken with Seaton. It is a shingly beach with some rock pool areas, and has the river running through the beach.

(This is the village of Seaton in Cornwall, there is also a town called Seaton in Devon.)

Another really good thing about Seaton beach is the **Beach Café**.

We had some scrumptious fish and chips, looked at the view, relaxed and downloaded our photographs to the laptop (The camera was full).

The café is decorated with driftwood, and drift rope. We would highly recommend a visit.

Fortified, we went back to the beach and had a small drink of wine in our new mugs to celebrate arriving at the coast. We are both from places near the sea, and sometimes we miss it. Derbyshire, where we live, is as far away from the sea as it is possible to be in England.

Next we drove to **Portwrinkle** beach. There is a steep walk to the beach which is rocky with dark sand and rock pools. We envied the people who lived in the house on the cliffs.

I had booked a bed and breakfast in Portwrinkle some weeks previously. We drove to the **B&B by the C** where we met Darryl and her husband who were very welcoming.

We had a lovely room with sea views, and decking outside. Darryl recommended going to the **Finnygook Inn** in Crafthole for a drink. This proved to be an excellent idea.

Nick the Fish was playing in the bar, and playing just our sort of music.

(You can find him on YouTube.)

The beer was also very fine. It was Sharp's Doom Bar bitter from the Rock Cornwall Brewery.

We wondered about the name Finneygook. Apparently Finny was a smuggler who ratted on the other smugglers to the Excise men. He was murdered at Bligers Well which is between Crafthole and Portwrinkle. His ghost or 'gook' is supposed to haunt the road.

"Do you think we will see the ghost?" I said to the driver.
"You never know," he said.

We didn't see the ghost.

We had a mug of the Horlicks provided by Darryl and went to bed – what a day!

Day 2

Sunday 13th May 2007

We awoke to very, very heavy rain. I had booked the room because of the stunning views shown on the internet. We had envisaged sitting out on the decking, drinking coffee and admiring the sea views in the sunshine.

Instead we watched great heavy drops of rain thudding on to the decking, and the sea through a sheet of water. It was a lovely room, a beautiful place to wake up, and we would like to go back again when it is sunny.

The decking had great views up the coast, down the coast, and over the sea. There were tables and chairs and there were fish ponds set into the decking. We went out with umbrellas to admire the views and the fish.

"Where are we staying tonight?" the driver asked.
"Um, I haven't brought the address," I said.

Oops. Fortunately the B&B had WiFi so the driver could use the laptop to check the address and postcode for the next stop.

Breakfast was very good. It was served in the conservatory where we could hear the rain drumming on the roof.

The B&B by the C may not be suitable for wheelchair users, as it has some difficult steps. However the proprietors told us that they could offer toast for the visually disabled – triangular for brown toast and oblong cut white toast. This was a suggestion made to the Chamber of Commerce, in response to the question of what they could offer disabled guests.

After breakfast we loaded the car in the rain and drove to **Crafthole**. We bought and posted some cards in the village shop (Remember the poor postman going up the steep track to deliver a postcard a day to Jim and Rosie in Wales?). The Archers was playing in the shop.

Then we drove back to the A38, through heavy rain, listening to the Archers. The B3247 was flooded and we drove through the flood water.

We stopped in **Downderry** to buy some highlighter pens to mark our maps. The driver drove over a curb to get into the car park, as he didn't realise it was there. This becomes significant later in the trip.

The village has a good-looking pub called the Inn on the Shore. It advertised 'Ensuite Bedrooms with Sea Views'. Just our sort of place we thought.

Apparently John Betjeman was fond of Downderry, and wrote lyrically of its charms. We have since been back, and stayed in the Inn on the Shore. Ask for Room One, it is a bit more expensive than the other rooms, but it has views straight out over the sea. You can lie in bed and watch the tide come in (or out).

We would have walked down to the shore, but the rain was still very heavy. I put my hand in my pocket.

"Look at this," I said to the driver.
"What is it?" he said.
"It's Darryl's key," I said.

Oops, oops. "We'll find somewhere to look up the address and post it back to her," the driver said.

We drove back along the River Seaton; it was very brown coloured and fast flowing compared to the day before.

There had been some serious rain that night and morning. Next we drove the roads past **Bonyalva** where there was grass growing in the middle of the road.

Bonyalva is shown in the Domesday Book with a population of four houses which include thirteen smallholders and 3 slaves.

I didn't know we had slaves but apparently it was common in Britain during the time the Domesday Book was written.

The roads were full of muddy water.

We went back to the A38 and then we stopped at Notter Bridge where the road crosses the River Lynher. It had stopped raining! We decided to go for a walk.

We found a DEFRA Conservation Walks notice, and it seemed to suggest a circular walk. I don't think that we interpreted the paths correctly, and we set off up a steep bank. We saw a badger set at the top, and we tried to find a path but there didn't seem to be one.

"I don't think this is a real path," said the driver.

We retraced our way down the bank, slowly, as it was very steep. We walked along the main path and found that there was a circular path, but we hadn't been on it. This had been difficult to make out from the sign.

If only we had brought a map.

It was a great walk, river, trees, bluebells and campion, and some impressive ivy vines.

It started raining again just as we got back to the car. Luckily we were parked just next to the **Notter Bridge Riverside Inn**, so we popped in for some coffee.

Our next stop was **Saltash Station**. We were intending to get a train back to Bodmin to look at all the places we had passed on the way. The station has really good views of the bridge over the Tamar River.

The timetables to travel one way are on one side of the station. The timetables for the return journey are on the other platform. There is a walk along the road and over a road bridge between platforms.

After some switching of sides we thought that we had about 40 minutes to wait for a train to Bodmin, and that the times would be alright to make the return trip to Saltash.

As we had some time to wait we walked down to **Mary Newman's cottage** which looked interesting...

...but there was a notice on the door saying that it was closed due to bad weather conditions

What a shame!

Mary Newman was married to Francis Drake in 1569. Her name has been linked with the cottage, although she may not have actually lived there. The cottage is fitted out as it would have been at the time she was alive, and it would have been interesting to have had a look. We will go back another time.

The driver went to buy some things in the town while I waited at the station in the sunshine.

When the driver came back he checked the train times again. He decided that we couldn't get to Bodmin and back after all, but he had a considerable amount of exercise moving between platforms, checking the timetables and making sure.

Because of this we decided to drive to Plymouth and get the train from there. We drove over the **Tamar Bridge** to Plymouth Station. It is a thrilling bridge to drive over. A suspension bridge opened in the early 1960s, and widened in 2001; it certainly is a spectacular part of the A38.

I had a cup of tea, the driver had some coffee and we both had some fruit cake while we waited for the train at Plymouth Station.

Then we rode the train to Bodmin, back across the **Royal Albert Bridge**. More stupendous views! This bridge was designed by Isambard Kingdom Brunel. It was opened in 1859 by Prince Albert, so I expect that is how it got its name.

Brunel's name is at either end of the bridge as a memorial, as he died the same year that it opened.

The train to Bodmin was a little train with decorated carriages, which gave you a real holiday feeling.

It also had single glass windows, so we were able to take some more pictures of all the places we had seen and stopped. It is about 26 miles between Plymouth and Bodmin. By car we had taken a day. It was much quicker on the train.

The train from Bodmin back to Plymouth was larger, and had two layers of glass which reflected back when you took pictures.

The driver took pictures through an open window including a picture of the A38 and the return to the Royal Albert Bridge.

From Plymouth Station we drove to **Kilbury Manor Farm** at **Buckfastleigh**. We had booked a room for the night and we were welcomed by our landlady, Julia.

It was a lovely room, self contained with our own front door. It gave us a chance to bring things in from the car and sort them out.

Julia recommended the Church House Inn at Rattery, which sounded good, so we went there for something to eat. We were going to drive there using the A38, but were diverted off because there had been an accident.

We had a very good meal:
Driver: Pheasant and Otter Ale from the Otter Brewery.
Me: Trout and Jail Ale from the Dartmoor Brewery.

The beer was served in jug glasses. I like a pint glass with a handle; it reminds me of my misspent youth. I expect they are more difficult to wash up than straight glasses.

The landlord told us some of the history of Church House Inns. Apparently, in the past, churchwardens provided the ingredients to make beer which was then sold, sometimes even in the church. The money raised was used for church repairs. The 'Church House' grew up as a place where church-goers gathered to drink church ales after the services.

The landlord also talked about the accident which closed the road and that the turn from Rattery on to the A38 was a black spot.

If you drive past the turning you can see how dangerous it might be if you approach the main road as if it were a slip road.

When we got back to our lovely room in Buckfastleigh we were accompanied inside by a cat which settled down on the driver's T shirt in the suitcase.

Unfortunately neither of us took a picture of the cat. This was a sad omission as he was a handsome fellow.

It was a very comfortable bed which was a welcome end to the second day.

Day 3

Monday 14th May 2007

We were woken up by the cat, which looked like a little lion with a ruff of longer hair around its neck. It was purring and kneading on the bedcover over the driver. I put him out so that we could get another hour's sleep.

When we woke up, we booked the Coombe Cross Hotel at Bovey Tracey for the next night. We did this using a combination of Sat Nav, the driver's mobile and the laptop. My Garmin Sat Nav showed us places to stay in the area and the driver accessed the internet using the phone as a modem for the laptop. Now the driver would have used his smart phone for everything, but this was in the primitive days of 2007.

We booked the hotel because it had a swimming pool. We also looked up the address for Darryl so that we could send her back the key. (Remember the key we forgot to return for the B&B by the C?)

Breakfast was very good.
Driver: Grapefruit, Full English
Me: Museli and yoghurt, salmon and scrambled eggs
This was accompanied by granary toast with real rasberry jam, delicious.

Julia told us the little lion cat was called George, that he didn't belong there, and certainly shouldn't have come into our room. We rather liked him.

We had a look at some of Julia's maps over coffee.

We loaded up the car, and I went to open the gate for the driver. As he started the car I heard it make a rattling noise.

"The car is making a rattling noise," I told the driver.
"Perhaps it needs some oil," he said.

Next stop was **Buckfast Butterflies and Dartmoor Otter Sanctuary**.

On the way there we drove under the A38, and so, of course, we had to take a picture.

Often during the trip we had to find somewhere to download photographs to the laptop. The cameras kept filling up. At this point the driver was still using a camera which took pictures on film, and I was using an Olympus digital camera.

We had a great time at the Otters and Butterflies, and took lots of pictures. The otters were enthralling.

So were the butterflies, the turtles and the plants. We also liked the leaf cutter ants.

In the gift shop we bought a T shirt with otters on, and a soft toy otter. The driver wears the T shirt, and our grandchildren play with the toy.

I have had a look at the Dartmoor Otters and Buckfast Butterfles website, and you can buy a cuddly otter online if you would like one.

At the railway station next to the Otters and Butterflies there were some old cars parked.

These evoked reminiscences of our youth and the cars our parents used to drive. There was even a steam train. This station is part of the **South Devon Steam Railway**. The railway line runs alongside the **River Dart**.

Next we went to the bridge over the River Dart and took some photographs of the bridge and the river. I took lots of photographs of the driver taking photos of the river and the bridge.

I was very disappointed to find that they were all out of focus. (Do you remember that the same thing happened when I photographed the driver taking photos of the River Seaton on Day 1?)

We drove on, and up to **Dartmoor** where we had a glorious walk in the sun.

What wonderful views and sunshine. After our walk we sat on the hill and had coffee from a thermos.

We had made the flask before we left the Kilbury Manor B&B. Those mugs I bought in Millets in Bodmin were coming in handy.

The driver tried to photograph swallows in the valley below.

This was his first attempt to photograph swallows on our journey, and the point at which he began to think that he needed a new camera.

Then we drove to **Badgers Holt** at **Dartmeet**.

Badgers Holt was an old fishing lodge, and is now a restaurant, somewhere to stay, and a tourist spot.

There were hens, ducks and geese to look at, and some tame chaffinches in the outside seating area. There were grey wagtails near the water. There was also a rather fine peacock.

This was a chance to be touristy, so we bought some postcards (for the trek up to Jim and Rosie) and some Dartmoor biscuits as presents when we went home.

The river was magnificent. Apparently Dartmeet has its name because the East Dart and the West Dart meet here. We took some pictures.

At last – I have managed to photograph the driver photographing a river. You can see the difference in quality of pictures taken by our cameras.

Next we drove to **Burrator Reservoir**, through lovely places and past Dartmoor ponies.

We drove over the bridge and marvelled at the dams. They were built in the 1890s and they are impressive constructions.

We drove back towards the A38, and had to be careful as there were sheep on the road. Just after we had passed the sheep we arrived at the village of **Sheepstor** which we felt was appropriate.

When we reached the A38, the driver decided that he really needed a new camera so we drove back towards Plymouth and found the Currys at **Plympton**.

After some deliberation, the driver bought a Pentax K110D. This has lots of features, and he seemed very pleased with it.

He takes real photographs, and these take longer than mine, because I just point the camera and click. Mind you, I do get a few out of focus pictures.

On the other side of the A38 there was a Sainsburys. We decided to buy some things for tea, so that we could eat in our room at the hotel. We felt like having an evening in.

On the A38, on the way to Bovey Tracey, the car started loosing power and making coughing sounds. The driver stopped at a garage just before the River Avon to put in some petrol and oil. The garage was opposite the **Woodpecker Inn**.

Further research on the internet has shown me that the Woodpecker Inn was demolished sometime in 2009.

We drove on to the **Coombe Cross Hotel** in Bovey Tracey. The car was still coughing.

The hotel was set in beautiful gardens. The hotel room was very pleasant. However, we realised that the decision to buy food for that evening was a fortuitous one, as we found this in the 'Information for guests'.

Dress Code: *Gentlemen are requested to wear at least a collared shirt for dinner. Smart casual dress is preferred around the hotel.*

We hadn't really packed anything 'Smart casual'.

Our good friend, John, had given us DVDs of the original BBC Survivors episodes which were originally shown on television in the 1970s. We had watched them when they were first on television, and remembered them as being very good. We planned to watch them again on the trip.

We had a picnic, drank wine and watched three episodes of Survivors. We had avocado, radishes, cucumber, potato salad, tomatoes, watercress and rocket salad, cheese, ham, bread, cashew nuts and red wine.

And so to bed...

I have looked up the Coombe Cross Hotel on Trip Adviser, and it was recently taken over by new managers (July 2012). We wish them well; we had a very enjoyable stay there.

Day 4

Tuesday 15th May 2007

Breakfast at the hotel was from 7am to 9am, and we were up too late to have it, and probably would not have been suitably dressed.

Over coffee we used the Sat Nav to search for Vauxhall garages, and booked the car into the Inchcape Vauxhall garage in Exeter.

Then we went for a swim in the hotel pool. It was very pleasant.

I like swimming very much. When I was a child I had an ambition to swim the English Channel. Now I am more sensible, although I have swum the Solent to the Isle of Wight.

I especially like that feeling of being the only person in a pool, and being the only one to ripple the calm surface.

Next we drove to the village of **Chudleigh Knighton** and went to the Post Office. We bought two postcards (one for the postman trekking up the path in Wales) and a Jiffy bag. There was a cat sitting in the Jiffy bag shelf, and I'm afraid we had to disturb him.

The people in the post office said that the cat didn't belong to them, but that he often came to visit. We posted the cards and used the Jiffy bag to post the keys back to Darryl in Portwrinkle.

"Look," the driver said. He was holding the key-card to the Coombe Cross hotel room.   Oops again. We drove back to the hotel to return it.

Then we drove to the garage in Exeter. Dave at the garage recommended the **Seven Stars** pub for lunch while he looked at the car. We selected Brie and Bacon Flatbreads at the Seven Stars and they were very good.

When we went back Dave at the garage (a very nice man) said that there was a problem with the catalytic converter, which would probably need replacing at some time but they didn't have one in stock.

Remember that curb the driver went over in Downderry on Day 2? It must have cracked the converter.

Dave said that they couldn't find anything else wrong with the car and that there was no charge. We told Dave about our journey, and he seemed to like the idea.

Our next stop was the **River Exe** in Exeter.

There was a shop which had bicycles and kayaks for hire. We asked about the kayaks, but because the weather had been so bad in the last few days the shop was not hiring canoes.

Apparently there was too much water.

However it was a good place to walk. It was here that I first photographed a mooring bollard.

Throughout the trip I took many pictures of bollards. I have a reasonable collection of bollard photographs now, if anyone should wish to see them.

"Why?" I can hear you ask. Well, I'm not really sure, perhaps it was because they were there, and they were all so different.

There were a number of nesting swans along the river. There were moorhens and ducks, gulls and a swimming dog. It was a springer spaniel I think, daft dogs, we used to have one.

We also walked around the **Exeter Ship Canal** basin which is adjacent to the river.

It was a very agreeable walk in the sunshine. Walking from, and back to the car we were next to parts of the impressive Exeter city walls.

When we came back to the car the driver said, "I can't find the camera bag."

"Where did you last see it?" I said.
"I may have left it at the garage," he said. We returned to the garage to pick up the camera bag.

Oops, oops, oops. There was a pattern emerging. We hoped that if things come in threes this would be the last time it happened.

There were many references to Topsham harbour on the boards around the river and canal basin, so we decided to go and have a look at it.

We found that there was a lido at Topsham, so we went for a swim. The water in the pool was chlorine free and it was great to swim in a heated pool outdoors. Two swims in one day!

We drove down to Topsham Quay and walked along the goat walk.

Apparently the name 'Goat Walk' was given when suggestions were asked for at a council meeting and one man said 'It's nowt but a bloody goat walk' and the name stuck.

From the goat walk you can see the waters of the **River Exe** and the **River Clyst** at their meeting point.

On the quay there is a pub called **The Lighter Inn**. We agreed that this would be a lovely place to have a drink and watch the boats in the harbour. However, we still needed to find somewhere to stay for the night, so we decided to move on.

At this point the A38 is the M5, and as we had already driven the M5 on the journey south, we took the **B3181** which follows the old A38 road. The B road crosses over the M5.

We drove to **Broadclyst**, and remarked at how many of the houses around the area were painted yellow. By the side of the road outside a pub called the **Red Lion Inn** there was a board advertising folk music on Wednesday evening.

If you are paying attention you will know that this was Tuesday evening, but they also offered accommodation, and after finding that they served Old Speckled Hen we decided to stay two nights. It would be relaxing not to have to pack up in the morning.

The Red Lion is a 16th century listed building. It is painted yellow, like many of the buildings in the area. We wondered why they were all this colour.

The Acland family owned most of the farms, cottages and land in the area and in 1944 bequeathed the estate to the National Trust. Is this a National Trust standard render colour?

The Red Lion doesn't so much list as bulge in some walls. Yet again we had found somewhere really good to stay.

We had a look at the church, which is from the 1600s and the stocks in the churchyard and then we walked down to the River Clyst. Broadclyst is a pretty village and it must have been quite different when the A38 used to come through it.

Then we had a magnificent dinner in the pub.
Driver: Pork Loin
Me: Gurnard (which is a type of fish).
We both had Apple and Rhubarb crumble, and as there was no driving involved, we poured a tot of brandy into the crumble. Delicious.

The dinner was accompanied by a number of pints of **Old Speckled Hen**. You may think that the beer is named after an elderly egg layer, but in fact it was named for an MG sports car owned by the MG factory.

The driver assured me that he was leaning over on purpose, so that I could take a picture of the Guinness sign. It was not a reflection of how much Speckled Hen he had enjoyed.

In the pub we met two walkers who were doing the Two Counties Way which is a walk of 56 miles from Taunton to Starcross on the Exe estuary.

They had just finished day 2 of a 3 day walk. I expect they needed the Hen as well.

There was a beautiful horse chestnut tree outside the pub. It was in full flower, and the flowers shone in the night light.

Another full day.

Day 5

Wednesday 16th May 2007

The room at the Red Lion was very comfortable, and had a lovely view. The bathroom was 'bijou' but adequate.

Breakfast was served in the conservatory, which had a glass roof and old brick/stone walls. There were fresh flowers on the table. We both had the very good fruit salad and full English. Also toast, jam, marmalade and coffee. Excellent.

Our landlady, Fiona, suggested that we should visit **Killerton House**, which was the manor house for the Acland family, and is now a National Trust property. So that was what we did, and walked around the gardens and the house.

Killerton has beautiful parkland, informal garden areas and more formal gardens, full of colour. They have obviously been planted, and since looked after, with a great deal of skill and affection.

They were amazing gardens, with views and even a giant redwood tree. (Sequoiadendron giganteum, also known as Wellingtonia after the Duke of Wellington.)

In the grounds there was an ice house pit that you could look at through a metal gate. On the wall next to the ice house was a sign which read:

THE ICE HOUSE
This was built in 1808 for Sir Thomas Acland. It is a brick lined pit over 20 feet deep with a drain at the bottom.

In 1809 30 men took five days to stow 40 tons of ice here, collected from the frozen pond and River Culm.

Insulated with straw, this was considered enough to supply the household for about three years. It was used in the kitchens and cellars for cooling rooms or soothing fevers.

We loved it all, but the most memorable part of our visit to Killerton House, and probably the thing that we remember with most affection from the whole trip is the **Bear's Hut**.

The sign inside the Bear's Hut reads:

This rustic summerhouse was built for Lydia, Lady Acland by her husband Sir Thomas Acland in 1808.

It wasn't <u>actually</u> built by Sir Thomas; it was built by the gardener and nurseryman, John Veitch, as a surprise for Lydia on the Acland's return from honeymoon.

What a romantic story, especially when you see the amazing amount of dedication that has gone into creating the hut. John Veitch was also the man responsible for planting the giant redwood tree.

The sign goes on to say:

It later became known as the Bear's Hut after their grandson, Gilbert, housed a pet bear here which he had shipped over from Canada.

Each of the three rooms is built of different materials, the floors with cobbles, log sections, and deer knuckle bones, the ceilings with basketry, matting and deer skins.

The stained glass in the hermit's chamber is sixteenth century Netherlandish.

We wondered what the bear made of the hut. We thought it was wonderful. If you get a chance you should go and see it for yourselves.

The house was full of lovely things, including a costume collection.

In the music room you can play the piano, so the driver had a go.

I had taken this picture before I realised that you were not allowed to take pictures in the house.

We had a cup of coffee in the Stable block tea-room, and wandered round the gift shop. Killerton House is a tremendous place to visit, and we would definitely go back to spend a whole day.

Next we drove to **Bickleigh Mill** at **Tiverton**, because it was shown on the map, and it was on the River Exe. The mill is mainly a shopping centre, but was a working mill up until 1960.

Near to a water wheel there was a white dove perched on an animal head and you could see baby doves in a nest in the bucket of the wheel. At the Mill we also saw the second peacock of our trip. The first one was at Badgers Holt at Dartmeet.

We walked along the river and took some photographs.

I took pictures of the driver taking photographs of the River Exe, but they were all out of focus. Again!

Near to the Mill is the **Devon Railway Centre and Model World**. This is a great place to take children, so we brought out our inner child for an hour or so. We went for a ride on the Narrow Gauge Railway and then marvelled at the skill and patience of the model makers, and pressed all the buttons to make the models work.

We played with the train set, and the driver spent a long time looking at the 0-4-0 industrial steam engine Pixie.

Pixie appears to have moved on, and I think it is now at the Leighton Buzzard Narrow Gauge Railway.

The models were all very impressive and there was even a little team of Morris dancers.

In the restored station buildings there is a tea room. We realised that we would be leaving Devon the next day, and so felt we should have a cream tea, with scones, jam and clotted cream. Very good.

From Bickleigh we drove to **Sampford Peverell**. There we found the **Grand Western Canal Country Park**, and a car park, so we stopped and walked along the canal.

The yellow flag irises were striking. Apparently they are an invasive species, but they did look good.

There were sheep on the other side of the canal and they seemed quite interested in us and walked along the other side of the canal with us for some of the way.

We spent some time watching a family of swans, until the male swan started to chase us off.

"They can break your arm, you know," I said to the driver.

Is this true?

I asked Steve Knight from the Swan Sanctury in Shepperton, Middlesex if it were true. He told me that it was theoretically possible but was extremely unlikely to happen.

Steve said that in the medieval times peasants would steal swans eggs and swans to eat from the landed gentry. Because of their diet their bones would be weak; unlike today where we get plenty of vitamins and calcium and our bones are stronger. The risk they took was getting a broken arm usually.

This is where the saying comes from and it has passed down through the ages.

So now you know. Thanks for your help Steve.

We liked this **Halburton** sign which showed you the way from the Canal path to the Pub, Shop, and Post Office.

If it had been earlier in the day we would probably have taken the path to the pub. Instead we walked back to the car and drove from Sampford Peverell towards **Sampford Arundel**.

In **Longwood Lane** we saw a hawk feeding on a rabbit in the middle of the road. These were very narrow lanes with high steep sides, and we remarked that it must be difficult for an animal to get out if they are in the road.

Sampford Arundel is on the A38, just past junction 27 on the M5. At this junction the A38 appears again with its own number. Sampford Arundel had been our destination target for this day.

We had been driving much smaller roads during the day, and now we drove back down the A38 to Junction 27 and then took the B3181 (the old A38 route) back to Broadclyst and the Red Lion.

We had dinner in the pub. It was, yet again, excellent.
Driver: Lamb Shank
Me: Chicken
both accompanied by very good vegetables and lots of Old Speckled Hen.

The driver played guitar with the two folk singers who were booked to play. They were brothers, Neil and Mac (the artist known as Mackenzie Moulton).

Two of Mac's paintings were on the walls in the pub and we had admired them the evening before. We had taken a photograph of one because we liked it so much. If we had been able to afford the painting we would have bought it.

There were also some people there from **Bradninch Folk Club**.

I went to bed, and left the driver playing.

Day 6

Thursday 17th May 2007

We had breakfast in the conservatory. As before we had fruit salad and full English with toast and coffee. Lovely. We packed up, said goodbye to the Red Lion and started back up the B3181 to pick up the A38 again.

We drove past **Diggerland** and the **Working Wool** museum, which looked interesting, but we decided to leave them for another time.

We crossed into Somerset at 11:07 and travelled the part of the A38 known as **Oldway Road**. Then we took the road to the **Wellington Monument**. We stopped in the car park and set off along the path to the Monument.

We were intrigued because we had driven the M5 many times, and the monument is clearly visible from the motorway. This was our chance to climb the 235 steps to the top.

We were disappointed to find that the monument was closed off by a fence. Apparently it is no longer safe to climb the steps to the viewing platform. We put our cameras through the fence and took some pictures of the base of the monument.

There was a National Trust information board in the area outside the monument. We thought that the information on the board was fascinating, the only things we knew about Wellington up to then was that he won the battle of Waterloo and that he invented the boots.

Arthur Wellesley came from a noble Irish family but not being the eldest it was his brother Richard who became a peer.

When Arthur distinguished himself in the victory over the French at Talavera during the Spanish Peninsular War he was duly enobled and had to select a title.

The Wellesley family had lived in Ireland since the 13th century but before that they came from Somerset and so a search revealed that the place in the county that most resembled his family name was Wellington, so on September 4th 1809 Arthur Wellesley became Viscount Wellington of Wellington and Talavera.

Following further triumphs he became the Duke of Wellington. He acquired an estate here but visited it only once in 1819: the townspeople bodily towing his carriage to the edge of the estate.

Following the Duke's victory at Waterloo the local gentry were quick to respond with plans to build this obelisque in his honour.

The foundation stone was laid in 1817 but the plans were too elaborate for the money available and it was left incomplete for many years until the death of the Iron Duke in 1852 when there was renewed vigour to complete the project.

Eventually the work was completed in 1892, the finished height: 175 feet.

We stood there and looked at the monument, and imagined some of the discussions which must have taken place in those 75 years between the start and the finish.

We wondered if the Duke had stood where we stood, (during his only visit to the area) looking at the foundation stone, and the progress made in two years.

Did he marvel at the views, or consider them with a military eye? The views are amazing, even from the base of the monument. Apparently in good weather you can see the Quantock Hills, the Bristol Channel, Dunkery Beacon on Exmoor, the Welsh mountains, the Mendips and Glastonbury Tor.

The National Trust board goes on to describe the efforts made to add cannons to the monument site. This is another story which makes you imagine the conversations of the people involved over the years. Was there worry, exasperation and humour?

The cannons' journey is remarkable. Although 24 cannon were promised, the first upset came in 1819 when 15 cannon arrived at Exeter Quay – and what was worse they were the wrong ones.

These cannon had been cast in Scotland, destined for Russia: they were certainly not used at Waterloo and what's more they were water rather than land cannon.

It was felt that they were not worth the expense of moving, so Exeter Quay was where they stayed. That is (there was a burn mark on the sign here so the next few words could not be seen but probably says 'until' and a date) ......when the cannon had to be sold to pay for the dock dues (space was required for timber).

A single brass cannon was sold for £64, ten iron ones were sunk as bollards, and the rest were buried.

In 1890 a West Country historian revived the question of transporting the cannon to the Wellington Monument, but once again it was felt that it was not worth it as the cannon had not been used at Waterloo.

In 1910 the cannon was dug up and mounted in a Park: all except four, which were once again offered to the Monument. This time they reached the Monument. Mounted on elm carriages, with iron wheels they must have looked a fine sight. But their glory was not to remain.

During World War II the cannon were removed for scrap, to help the war effort. It was believed they were never used but buried on the cliffs at Watchet (a thorough search organised by the Rotary Club could find no trace). The Wellington Rotarians were determined to restore this historic feature to the Monument, so they went back to Exeter Quay; where they were delighted to find 3 cannon inscribed with "Carron 1789". One of the cannon was donated to the Monument and so a special carriage was made.

When we were there you couldn't really see the cannon because of the wall around the Monument. I believe that the wall has been replaced with a wire fence, and that there are plans to restore the Monument, but once again, I expect, it will be a question of funds.

The information in the National Trust sign and the panoramic views were the best parts of our visit to the Monument. Also, the sun was shining!

There are some beautiful beech woods around the Monument. We walked through the woods until the path became too steeply down-hill for me to manage (I have some osteoarthritis in my knees).

Back at the car park we had coffee from a thermos flask we had made up at the Red Lion. Those mugs from Millets were useful again.

It became warm enough for the driver to take his jumper off while he consulted the maps. Hooray!

Travelling on along the A38 we passed **The Worlds End** pub, which is an impressive building, and was a coaching inn. We speculated about making another trip one day, visiting coaching inns along the way. Possibly it might be better to choose a shorter road for this project?

We did wonder about the name of the pub. Were Devon and Cornwall once beyond the end of the world? Or is it the other way round?

A little further on we passed **Sheppy's Cider Museum**, which looked worth a visit, but we put it on our 'next time' list.

We drove along the A38 through Taunton, stopping briefly at a supermarket to pick up some supplies. The name of the A38 to the east of Taunton is **Toneway** and it roughly follows the course of the River Tone.

The road crosses the **River Tone** near the hamlet of **Bathpool** (Bathpool in Somerset, not to be confused with Bathpool in Cornwall which is near the River Lynher).

We drove on to the **Bridgewater and Taunton Canal** and stopped in the Bathpool car park.

We walked along the canal path, back towards Taunton. Some of the places we passed were industrial, but it was a very good walk. The path is excellent, and we'd like to cycle there one day.

We saw a blackcap (the bird, not the hat) in the bushes by the side of the path and also disturbed a grass snake which was taking in the sunshine on the path.

The driver took photographs of dragonflies over the water, and we have a modest collection of pictures in which you can just make out a blue streak. We saw duck, swan and moorhen families. The ducklings, cygnets and young moorhens were enchanting.

We found a stone showing information on Neptune.

There is a model of the solar system along the canal! This is the Somerset Space Walk, which has stones set in proportional sizes and distances apart. It has two models of each planet, which are spread out either side of the sun at Maunsel Lock. Each set covers a distance of 6.8 miles.

The canal comes close to the River Tone in some places and you can walk between the two.

We also found an intriguing post sign with the words 'Childrens Wood' carved into it. There was a board nearby which was headed '**The Children's Wood**' and gave us the following information:

The Orchard

Traditional orchards have been part of our landscape and cultural heritage for many centuries. During this time, wildlife has adapted to take advantage of the benefits orchards offer.

Cider became part of the farm labourers wage, making up 15% of his income. The orchard became part of our culture through ceremonies such as wassailing, which was performed to drive away evil spirits and ensure a good crop the following year.

The sight of Taunton Vale, filled with apple trees in blossom; an area renowned for its cider, was said to be spectacular. However, by the 1940's the importance of orchards began to decline with the introduction of new agricultural techniques. The orchards were grubbed out to make way for improved grassland and arable land. In 1874 Somerset had 24,000 acres of orchard. By 1973 this had been reduced by almost 90% to 2,499 acres. This has been matched by a decrease in the number of varieties of apple, with many local varieties lost. The character of orchards has also changed from 20-30 foot standard trees with spreading branches, to 10 foot bush trees grown closer together to increase acreage yield.

Childress Wood orchard contains nine traditional apple trees donated by Taunton Cider and planted in March 1994 with the help of pupils from St Augustine of Canterbury School, Priorswood.

I found some further information on the internet saying that there was a plan to plant another tree for each baby born in the area. What a splendid idea.

Along side the canal at Firepool we took a picture of a building which we found intriguing. It has **BRITISH RAILWAYS** painted at the top of the structure. I have looked for information on it, and it is a Grade II listed building, it was a pumping station for steam trains and it was built on the site of some medieval lime kilns. The top bit of the building is a large water tank. There are plans to make the building into a restaurant. We would have welcomed a cup of tea at this point.

We had a look at the lock at Firepool. This is where the canal joins the River Tone, and the canal finishes. Unfortunately this was as far as we could go as the footpath ahead was closed. So we turned and walked back to Bathpool.

The driver managed to get a picture of a dragonfly on the way back. He was very pleased.

There were elder flowers blooming in the hedges at the side of the paths. In Derbyshire I associate the elder flowers with June and hawthorn with May. The driver pointed out that we were 'south' so perhaps they bloomed earlier here. I always think of the line 'Elder flowers like foam' in the Cicely Fox Smith poem 'Home, Lads, Home' when I see them.

By the time we were back at the Bathpool lock I was desperate for a loo, so we asked the lock-keeper if we could use his. He was very friendly, said yes, and told us a bit about the Neptune block that we had seen and that it was a solar system trail. He told us that the Sun was at **Maunsel Lock** and that there was a tea room at the lock.

This was welcome news, but we decided go by car, rather than walk along the canal. We drove to the lock and on the way there we saw a stoat with a mouse in its mouth running across the road.

The tea room at the Lock was remarkable. We had coffee and some very good cake. We sat in the sun and looked at the water and the boats and the wild life. It was very relaxing, and we felt that we deserved the rest.

The wild life came quite close, and a robin was obviously very used to people visiting his perching area, as he was landing right on our table.

We bought a couple of tin mugs with canal boat designs in the shop. We also found Mars at the Maunsel Lock. We had thought to find the sun, but didn't realise at the time that the centre of the solar system is at **Higher Maunsel Lock**. Now that we know, we will go back and do the whole solar system one day.

Our next destinations were Huntspill and Highbridge on the A38. From here we drove along the coast road through Burnham on Sea, Berrow and Brean. We had planned to go and look at the sea, but the car was coughing much more and a warning light came on.

We decided to drive to the Premier Travel Lodge in Weston-super-Mare, stay the night and book the car into a garage in the morning. We discussed what we would do if we couldn't continue with the dear old thing. We thought we would get the train back home to Derbyshire, and then drive down in my car so that we could carry on. Then I would have been the driver and the writer!

Our goal for the day had been to stay around the Huntspill/Pawlett area. Our travels around Weston-super-Mare took us onto other A roads, which was against our self imposed rule. (But are rules made to be broken?)

I knew the Premier Inn at Weston as I had stayed there before for work, and there was a Vauxhall Garage in the town. Premier Inns are generally reliable and comfortable. There are two other things going for this one as far as we are concerned. Firstly it has a swimming pool next door. We booked in and went for a swim. Secondly it has a reasonable pub with good beer on the other side.

The Pavilion is a Beefeater chain pub, and I have always had meals which were very acceptable there. And it serves **Butcombe Bitter** which is a very good pint from the Butcombe Brewery.

We both had cod and chips and a few pints of the excellent bitter. We also lost £5 very rapidly playing the fruit machine. I said that I hadn't really played one before, and the driver said he would show me how it was done…

Later we drank red wine in bed and watched two episodes of Survivors.

Day 7

Friday 18th May 2007

We had tinned fruit salad for breakfast, followed by a bit of togetherness.

In the car park of the travel inn we saw a yellow stripy bird. Neither of us was aware of having seen one like it before, and we said, "Look at that bird." and, "What is it?" We looked it up in the bird book and decided that it was a siskin.

We drove to St Georges Garage with the car coughing and the warning light on.

The garage man (Andy) said that he thought it was the Cat, and put the car up to have a look. We had brought a Scrabble set and started a game.

The Cat was the problem (part of the exhaust system apparently).

The people in the garage ordered a replacement and said that we should come back between 3 and 4pm. This was obviously going to take longer than a game of Scrabble so we thought we would go and find the sea.

We walked to the beach, but the sea was out. We walked to the **Grand Pier** and walked along it. Although it was quite nice, we felt that 'Grand' was going a bit far.

My knees were beginning to feel the strain of all this walking so we paid for a trip back on the little yellow train that was running along the pier.

It appears that the pier is now much grander than when we visited it in 2007. In 2008 it was bought by new owners who spent money on renovation. Their work was undone by a fire which destroyed the pavilion, but it has since been rebuilt and has many attractions.

The owners were awarded MBEs in the 2012 Birthday Honours list for their work in restoring the pier.

The sea really does go out a very long way.

We walked along the sea front and stopped at a pub advertising cream teas. I'm afraid to say that it really wasn't very good. The scones were very dry and the jam and the butter were in little containers, and of poor quality.

We carried on walking along the front. There are some curious weathering patterns in some of the stones of the sea wall.

It looks as though there is seaweed on top of the wall in this picture, but the stone has weathered away to leave these markings.

We walked to the **Birnbeck Pier**. It was closed, and the weather was turning grey. The poor old pier looked very sad.

We went into a corner shop and bought some postcards and newspapers. As we came out it started raining, and we abandoned the attempt to be tourists and went into the pub across the road.

We had a beer. We looked out across the bay through the rainy windows. We read the papers. The driver did the Circle Sudoku in the Times (I don't think that he has done a Sudoku before or since). We looked at the fish in the pub's rather magnificent fish tank.

It was still raining heavily, so we ordered a taxi back to the garage. Car fixed!

We drove back to Highbridge to pick up the A38 where we left it. We drove to Upper Langford along the A38 then took the roads off to Shipham, and from there to **Cheddar Gorge**.

I had been to the cheese factory tour before, and was keen to go again, this time with the driver. I had told him about the song that they played during the tour, "English cheddar, gorgeous, gorgeous" which I think comes from a Cheese Council advert from the 1970s. I had even sung it to him, and I could tell that he couldn't wait. Do they still play it?

We were too late for the tour, but just in time to buy some cheese from the shop. We walked around the area at the bottom of the gorge, ate the cheese and took some photographs. Then we drove up the gorge and marvelled at its height and beauty. We stopped to take more photos.

The Cheddar Gorge website has some stunning views of the gorge. Our pictures didn't really do it justice, but the pictures at their website are worth a look.

As we drove on we saw some goats on the side of the gorge. I always find it exciting that goats can climb such steep areas. We drove through the gorge along Charterhouse Lane, to Shipham and then back to the A38.

Between Langford and Redhill we passed a sign for the **Butcombe Brewery Shop**. This was a place that we would like to visit, but time was getting on and we were booked into the **Old Passage Inn** in **Arlingham** for the night. If you are following the journey on a map, then you will find that Arlingham is a big leap up the A38, considering the pace of the journey so far.

We had discovered the Old Passage Inn on a previous exploration of the peninsula in the River Severn, and thought it would be a great place to stay. I had booked two nights there before we set out.

The driver stopped on the way to take pictures of the view from the A38 over Bristol and the magnificent Clifton Suspension Bridge. This is another structure designed by Isambard Kingdom Brunel.

Following the signs for the A38 in Bristol took us near the bridge and along the **River Avon** for a while.

I said to the driver "Didn't we cross the River Avon in Devon?"

"It isn't the same Avon, there is more than one," he said. "The word 'Avon' means 'River' so they are all called River River."

How many River Avon are there in Britain?

In England there are
River Avon (Devon)
River Avon (Warwickshire)
River Avon (Hampshire)
River Avon (Bristol)
Avon Water (Hampshire)

In Scotland there are
River Avon (Falkirk)
River Avon (Strathspey)
Avon Water, tributary of the River Clyde

In Wales there is
River Avon, which is an occasional anglicisation of River Afan

We drove on to Arlingham and the Old Passage Inn.

The room in the Old Passage Inn was very exciting with lots of features. It had two windows, both with views over the River Severn. The side window also had views of the Helipad.

There was a CD player, a television, a DVD player and a bowl of cupcakes. There were some lovely objects to look at and touch.

There was a glass wall between the bathroom and the rest of the room. The room also had a microwave, a toaster, a kettle, and a fridge and all the ingredients you need for a do-it-yourself breakfast.

his was the most expensive place that we stayed during our trip, and it was definitely worth it. Apart from all the other reasons the view from the main window was straight out over the river, and we could lie in bed and look out at it.

The Old Passage Inn isn't a pub; it's a fish restaurant with three rooms that you can book to stay the night. We ate in the restaurant.

It is fairly pricey, so this was a bit of a treat.
Both: Olives in sauce which was labelled as pre-starter.
Driver: Watercress and potato soup with smoked haddock followed by Monkfish
Me: Smoked salmon and caviar followed by Sea bass

After dinner we went for a short walk along the Severn in the dusk. Then we retired to bed, drank red wine and watched some more episodes of Survivors.

Day 8

Saturday 19th May 2007

We sat in bed, having breakfast, and watched the tide come in along the River Severn. We had cereal, muesli, yoghurt, juice and toast, and the river rising. Amazing.

There was a folder in the room which had a page telling you about the river:

The River Severn
Known as Sabrina during Roman Times, the river rises in Plinlimmon, Mid Wales. The catchment area is 1.8 million square miles and rain that falls in Wales takes 3 days to reach the Old Passage Inn.

Before the last Ice Age the river flowed into the bay of Liverpool, it now falls 2500 feet in the first 5 miles and then drops 500 feet over the next 215 miles. The river flows through Shrewsbury, Bridgnorth, Stourport, Worcester, Gloucester and into the Irish Sea beyond Bristol. It is Britain's longest river and has Salmon and Elvas as edible fish.

The Severn Bore
On each tide a wall of water is created about 2½ miles downstream when the seawater hits a large stony bank. The height of the wall depends on the time of month and year. The largest coincides with spring tides in April and September, up to 5-6 feet of water in a wall.

Newnham on Severn
On the opposite side of the river from here is Newnham. A small Georgian town which once was the ferry point at this river crossing. Prior to this a 'Bar' provided safe wading across the river. (Tides & Bores permitting!)

In 602AD St Augustine walked across the river to meet Welsh Christians and before that the Romans often used this crossing.

Next we drove back along the A38 to the **Bristol Harbour**. We stopped in a car park on the **Princes Wharf**.

We walked along the wharf and looked at the trains and cranes and the harbour. We took pictures of lots of boats, including the **Matthew** which was built as a replica of John Cabot's boat in which he sailed to America in 1497.

There was a board on the harbour which gave information about the River Avon Trail. It had this information about the Bristol Harbour:

In the medieval period England produced something that the rest of Europe wanted - fine quality wool. Bristol grew rich from the trade.

The main import was wine from France but Bristol merchants also traded with much of Europe's western seaboard. They brought salt and iron from Spain and fish from Scandinavia.

It was in pursuit of fish (principally cod) that Bristol seamen first went to Iceland and then to Newfoundland. It is widely held that Bristolians were in North America years before Columbus or Cabot made their voyages.

It is a Bristol joke that when Cabot arrived in Newfoundland in 1497, he was the only member of the crew who hadn't been there before.

The Bristol Harbour is big. It soon became apparent that the best way to see it would be by boat, so we stopped at the Bristol Packet jetty. There was a little time to wait for the next tour, so we bought ice creams from a van and sat in the sun waiting for the boat.

The tour was brilliant, well worth the money. We both took masses of pictures of bridges and buildings and boats (including some model boats) and the **SS Great Britain**.

The Great Britain is another of Isambard Kingdom Brunel's designs. It is a museum, and we were tempted but we decided to leave a tour round her for another visit.

After the boat trip we walked further along the quay and admired sculptures and sailing dinghies. On the way back along the wharf I increased my collection of photographs of bollards...

...and the driver played with the trains.

We stopped at **Brunel's Buttery** and had a bacon sandwich and a cup of coffee.

The driver decided that it was time to go and we went back to the car. I could tell that he was a man with a purpose as he drove away from Bristol and up the A38. He pulled into a pub car park in **Alveston**.

It was there that I realised that it was Cup Final day. It was Manchester United v Chelsea. The driver went to university in Manchester, and is a Manchester United supporter.

I became a football widow while he watched the match in **The Cross Hands of Alveston**.

I found a Londis shop and bought postcards, wine, provisions, and a TV listings.

I looked up the start time for Doctor Who that evening (We are both Doctor Who fans).

I took a photograph of the signs to the A38...

...and a photograph of a cricket match.

After that I went back to the pub. Chelsea had won. "It's only a game," I said. It didn't seem to help.

We decided to explore some more around the Severn, so drove through Thornbury, where we saw signs to Thornbury Castle.

We went up the drive and realised that it was a hotel, and that it had valet parking, so was probably out of our price range for this trip. It was an impressive place from the outside.

I have looked up the hotel, it is a 500 year old building, once belonging to Henry VIII, and it looks a beautiful place to stay.

Next we drove to **Littleton on Severn** which has an area of the village called Whale Warf, because a whale was stranded there in 1885.

Then for completeness we drove to **Oldbury on Severn** and looked at the decommissioned nuclear power station.

We drove back to **Whale Warf**, parked and walked along the Severn, taking pictures of the Severn Bridge and the power station.

On the way back to Arlingham we were distracted by a sign directing us to The Slad.

"What is a Slad?" I said.
"I don't know," said the driver.

So we went to have a look. We are not really sure if we found it. It might be a sign to the village of Slad, (where Laurie Lee used to live) or to the Slad Brook.

What we did find was a board headed **BRISTOL'S TIME GAP.** It showed information about:

Rocks A
Carboniferous Limestones
...sediments laid down on the sea floor 350 million years ago...
and
Rocks B
Dolomitic Conglomerate
...of Triassic age and is between 240 and 220 million years old...
   ...The boundary between the two discordant sets of sediments is known as an angular unconformity and represents a time gap of at least 50 million years.

Looking at the Time Gap made us slightly late for the start of Doctor Who when we arrived back at the Old Passage Inn. It was quite appropriate really.

Afterwards we watched the Doctor Who Confidential on BBC3, and then picnicked in our room with the provisions we had bought, and the contents of our breakfast cupboard. The driver experimented with taking pictures of the river, the moon, and the lights of Newnham.

Another incredibly full day over.

Day 9

Sunday 20th May 2007

A leisurely start at the Old Passage Inn. I went down to sit by the river. It was so quiet and peaceful there. We realised that we hadn't taken any pictures of the restaurant when we ate there on Friday evening, and we asked if we could take some now. The man we spoke to suggested that he take a picture.

He also took a picture of us sitting outside. These are the only two photographs of us together on the trip.

In the gardens of the Inn, in addition to the Helipad, there was a blue model of the **Statue of Liberty**, as well as a very sociable puppy.

We packed up and left the Old Passage Inn and headed for **Sharpness.** We found that there were docks and the beginning of a very big canal there.

We watched a dutch cargo ship, the **Arklow Rock** go through the lock. It was a very, very big lock and it took a long time for the water level to change.

From the picnic area at the docks we could see back to the power station at Oldbury on Severn.

On a notice board you could see times of arrivals and departures of boats coming into the docks, and the heights of the tides.

There was also an advert for excursions from Sharpness on the Waverley Paddle Steamer. I would have liked to have taken a trip on the Waverley. It is the only paddle steamer in the world which still takes passengers to sea. I think she does excursions from other ports around Britain, and we have since seen her sailing out of Felixstowe.

When I was very small my grandmother took me on one of the paddle steamers which operated between Portsmouth and Ryde. It is one of my earliest memories and I remember it as being exciting, the sea was quite rough, and I don't think that all the passengers enjoyed the trip.

The docks are very much a working area, and a strong contrast to the Exeter and Bristol dock areas. We enjoyed sitting in the sunshine and watching the slow traffic. I also increased my bollard collection.

Our next destination was the nature reserve at **Slimbridge**. This was one of the few places that we planned to visit in advance of starting out. Mostly we just happened on places along the way.

I had looked up Slimbridge before we left home, and knew that the reserve was founded by Sir Peter Scott. I knew that he, and the Wildfowl and Wetlands Trust have been responsible for saving species of wildfowl from extinction.

We like ducks, geese and other water birds. We have two indian runner ducks that roam around our garden at home and help to keep the place 'tidy'. So a trip to the wetlands at Slimbridge was a must.

The canal with the big lock at Sharpness also runs through the village of Slimbridge and then goes on to Gloucester. Just in front of the wetlands centre there is a bridge called **Patch Bridge** which crosses the canal.

Our first stop at the Reserve was the café, where we had coffee and sandwiches. It had been thirsty work watching that ship through the lock. Then we wandered around the ponds and saw and fed ducks, geese and swans of many colours.

The swan with the yellow beak is a Bewick's swan. We learned that they have unique different patterns on their beaks, and that Sir Peter Scott had realised this in 1964, and used the knowledge to study the swans.

There was a very friendly goose; a Hawaiian Goose, also called a Nene. This was one of the species which had been rescued from the brink of extinction and re-introduced to Hawaii.

The flamingos were fascinating. Apparently Slimbridge is the only place in the world where you can see all six species of flamingo.

There were lots of 'Ahh' moments during the afternoon with ducklings, goslings, cygnets, and coot and moorhen babies.

We had a chance to see coot and moorhen close up (and out of the water).

We remarked on the coot's feet. It has little pads on its feet, which are quite curious, (apparently they are known as lobes) while the moorhen has feet much more like a chicken.

We thought about it and you see moorhen often on land, and coot are generally swimming.

We went to the Kingfisher hide and sat there for ages. The driver would very much like to see a kingfisher, but there weren't any about. There were jackdaws and we watched the jackdaw babies being fed.

Leaving the Wetlands centre we crossed the **Patch Bridge** and took some pictures of the canal.

There was an advert for a place to hire bicycles on the canal, and we thought that a short cycle would be good. We drove to the cycle hire place, but it was already closed. It was a shame – it was only half past four. Then we saw a sign that said that you needed a licence to cycle on the towpath, so perhaps it was just as well. I don't think that you need a permit anymore.

We explored the A38 up towards Gloucester and turned off to look at the canal again just before Quedgeley. We found a pub called **The Pilot** with views over the canal and thought that it looked like a good place to stop, so we had a pint there. In retrospect this was not a good idea.

We drove on to Gloucester docks. It was here that we realised that **we were TETCHY**. We were tired and dehydrated. We had been holidaying with attitude for ten days (if you count day zero). We had been walking around the wetland ponds in the sun, and had only had a coffee and a beer since the morning.

So Gloucester docks didn't really get explored. We phoned and booked a room at the Premier Travel Inn in Twigworth and then drove back to the Pilot for something to eat.

We drank fizzy water, and I forgot to write down what we had for dinner. But I remember that it was a fine location to relax a bit.

Afterwards we thought about walking along the canal, but my knees were sore, and we were tired, so we just looked at it.

We will come back one day and cycle the towpath, and possibly take our kayaks out.

We drove on to the Premier Travel Inn at **Twigworth**. We have both stayed in Premier Inns many times, from Newcastle to the Isle of Wight and most places in between. As I said on Day 6 they are generally reliable and comfortable.

Twigworth Premier Inn was having an off night. There wasn't anyone in reception when we arrived (this isn't uncommon when you arrive late, and usually someone comes in from the bar very quickly).

It did take quite a while here, and to be honest, when someone arrived it wasn't a great improvement on unattended.

The room we were given didn't seemed to have been cleaned properly, there was an empty beer glass and a used ashtray in the room.

I went back to reception to check whether this was really an empty room, or if someone would come back from the bar to disturb us.

We were shown another room, but decided to stay where we were. We were very tired, and the thought of moving everything again was too much. We bought a pint of beer each in the Twigworth pub, and took it back to our room.

We watched an episode of Survivors. This seemed appropriate, because surviving just about summed it up that night.

I'm sure that Premier will have sorted out any problems at this hotel long ago. We were just unlucky. I see from the internet that the pub next door called The Twigworth has been taken over and is now called The Oakwood.

It was a shame that it coincided with us having reached a low point.

Day 10

Monday 21ˢᵗ May 2007

We were woken up by a knocking noise. It sounded like someone knocking on the door and was quite startling, but it turned out to be a man fixing tables outside in the pub garden.

The driver said that he had been dreaming about a woodpecker before he woke up. "Have you ever seen a woodpecker?" I said. "No," he said.

We downloaded our photographs to the laptop. Usually we did this in the evening, but the last night we hadn't felt like doing anything. We drank coffee and watched some more episodes of Survivors. We were having a rest! Then we experienced a little togetherness.

We phoned Cheltenham Lido, as we had planned to make an excursion to swim, but it was closed for refurbishment. This was a disappointment because we had been looking forward to it. I have swum in the Lido a few times, and it is great, especially on a school day in May when there are not many people in.

Finally we packed up again and drove along the A38 to **Norton**, and then to **Bishop's Norton** and then to the River Severn again along Wainlode Lane.

Here we found **The Red Lion**.

This was an amazing find and we remember it with fondness. We have been back several times, going out of our way to see it again.

It has a caravan and camping park and we have often said that we should go and spend a few days there.

The tables across the road have a wonderful view of the Severn. You can sit and watch the narrow boats passing and make friends with the ducks and sparrows.

We wanted to go for a walk, so we parked in the car park and asked the landlord if this would be alright, as we were going to come back for some lunch. He said yes. We walked down-river (which was uphill into cliffs by land).

From here we could see along the Severn and across the fields to the hills.

The path went through woods and open land, and the world was rich with elderflowers, white and pink dog roses, bramble flowers, cowslips, buttercups, cow parsley (or was it hemlock?), clover and all around was lush and green.

We walked until the path became too muddy, because we weren't wearing our wellies. Our spirits were high again.

We walked back to the Red Lion and had lunch, no beer this time, fizzy water and coffee to drink. What a marvellous place to have lunch.

Afterwards we walked up river a little way and then found a small watercourse leading away from the river with a footpath alongside. We decided to walk this and see where it went.

The meadows were full of buttercups and there were more dragonflies (they may have been damselflies – we are not too clear on the identification) than we had ever seen before.

The driver took 57 photographs of them.

I took 5 photographs and I was quite pleased with mine until the driver showed me his.

We carried on walking and taking pictures through some really beautiful places. We discovered that we were in **Coombe Hill Nature Reserve** because we found a board telling us about it. 'Restoration of a major Severn Vale wetland' the board said. We later learned that at some points we were walking along the disused Coombe Hill Canal.

We saw grasshoppers and beetles and bugs, swans and cygnets, snails and ducks, and many different grasses and flowers.

I know that in June and July of 2007 there were devastating floods in Gloucestershire, and I expect that many of the plants and creatures we saw that day were terribly affected. But while we were there we felt we had discovered a garden of Eden.

We found some ponds with holes in the bank. "Do you think they could be kingfisher holes?" I asked the driver.

"Could be," he said, so we sat down and watched for a while. No kingfishers, but we heard a knocking noise, very like a man fixing a table in a pub garden.

"Do you think that could be a woodpecker?" I asked the driver.
"Could be," he said and went to look for it.

It was. A greater spotted woodpecker. It flew away, and then came back, but then flew away before the driver could get a picture. First the dream, and then the actual bird. A remarkable coincidence, so we remarked on it.

We walked back to the Severn and spent some time watching the swallows dipping over the river and along the bank. The driver spent a while trying to photograph them, and ended up with a lot of pictures of where the swallows had been a second ago.

We had another fizzy water at the Red Lion. We were not taking any risks of becoming dehydrated that day.

We drove up the A38 and found the other end of the Coombe Hill Nature Reserve. There is a small car park at this end.

Next we drove towards Tewkesbury and up the Gloucester road. We turned off to go along **Lower Lode Lane** for another look at the River Severn.

We met a man with a canoe, and a friendly white cat. The driver took some more blurry pictures of swallows.

We drove on to **Tewkesbury** and looked at the Mill Buildings at the Junction of the Severn and the Mill Avon. We walked across the bridge to the island. The island is called the Ham and is an area of common land between the rivers Avon and Severn.

This is the **River Avon (Warwickshire)**. River Avon (Devon) was Day 3 and River Avon (Bristol) was Day 7.

There was a notice board on the bridge, giving information about the **Abbey Mill**:

A mill was constructed on this site around 1190 for the Priory of Tewkesbury which had been established in 1102 by Robert Fitzhamon, Lord of Gloucester. It was operated by Benedictine monks and supplied by local farmers.

The mill was rebuilt in 1793 and had 4 wheels to power the mill stones. Healings Flour Mill, at the northern end of the Ham, was constructed in 1865 and enlarged in 1889. It is said that this led to the decline of Abbey Mill which eventually ceased operation in 1920.

Just round the corner from the bridge we found **The Bell Hotel** and I went in to ask if they had a room for the night. They did, and so we booked it, and had dinner there.
Driver: Duck followed by Strawberries and cream
Me: Asparagus pancakes followed by Bread and butter pudding

This was washed down with a few pints of excellent Abbot Ale from the Greene King Brewery. It seemed appropriate as we had just been reading about the Abbey Mill. It was all very good, especially the bread and butter pudding.

We had a window table, and just across the road from where we were sitting there was sign-post with 'Severn Way' pointing in both directions. That seemed appropriate too.

And so to bed.

And - it was a four poster!

Day 11

Tuesday 22nd May 2007

Coffee in bed was in mugs provided by the hotel. Not just any mugs, these had a picture of the Bell on them.

We had breakfast at the Bell, there was fruit, yoghurt and toast and:
Driver: Full English breakfast
Me: Egg, tomato and hash browns
It was very good.

Tewkesbury has lots of Tudor buildings and the Bell hotel is one of them.

I think that when we stayed there it was independently owned and now it is owned by Old English Inns. It was a place we would like to stay again.

We walked into the town, and took pictures of timber framed buildings.

We took the driver's earlier camera films into a shop to get them developed onto a CD. Remember that he had an old style camera when we started out? It wasn't until Day 3 that he bought his digital camera.

It would take a while for the CD to be ready, so we went back to the Abbey Mill to catch a ferry. It was a lovely warm day, and we had seen the ferry timetable the night before.

The ferry called the Avon Belle II went from Tewkesbury, stopped at River Walk and then at the Fleet Inn at Twyning. We could stay at the Fleet for lunch and catch another ferry back.

The first part of the boat trip was on the Mill Avon. The waterway was man-made in the 12th Century by the Benedictine monks from the Abbey. It was built to send water to the wheels at the Abbey Mill.

We went past **Healings Mill** which used to make flour and past **Tewkesbury Lock**. The lock links the River Avon (Warwickshire) and the River Severn together.

The boat took us under King John's Bridge. The bridge was originally built for King John in the 12th Century and it is another view of the A38 because the road goes over the river on the bridge.

We went past weirs and boats, sheep and swans. The ferry dropped us off at **The Fleet Inn** in **Twyning**.

Apparently the name Twyning means 'between the rivers.'

I haven't written down what we had for lunch. I expect that it was probably a sandwich, coffee and water; we wouldn't have been very hungry after the breakfast at the Bell.

It was another great place to sit in the sun and look at the river. While we were there we heard a cuckoo calling, and we watched baby wagtails being fed. There were guinea pigs in a pen, and we saw a baby dove in the dovecot.

On the way back along the **Avon** we saw dozens of dark blue dragonflies, they were so dark that they looked black. We also saw a heron standing on the bank.

It was a beautiful river trip. Tewkesbury and the surrounding areas were very badly affected by the floods later in 2007. The Fleet Inn was flooded, the Bell was surrounded by water, and the Avon Belle II was put up for sale. She has been renamed as Look Ahead II (which was originally her name) and she cruises on the River Fal in Cornwall. I don't know if you can still take a ferry up to Twyning.

We went back into Tewkesbury to pick up the photo CD. We also bought some T-shirts, a tripod for a camera and some china fish in a charity shop. "China fish?" I can hear you ask, but I have no idea why we wanted them, and we no longer have them.

We drove south down the Gloucester road to pick up the A38 where we had left it the day before. Then we drove north up the A38 towards Worcester.

We drove through Severn Stoke and Clifton and then took a turning off to the left onto the Old Road South. We drove down to Lane's End where I took a picture of a garage with a blue clock set into the brickwork.

We drove back down towards the A38 and towards Worcester again. We passed the oast houses at Baynall and remarked at the funny shape.

"What is an oast house?" I said.
"I'm not sure," the driver said.
"I'll look it up," I said.

Apparently an oast house is (or was) used for drying hops. The reference source I used said that they were examples of vernacular architecture.

I had to look up 'vernacular architecture' as well, and found that it is a form of building which evolves from local requirements and the materials available to the builders.

Somewhere in these travels the driver took a picture of the Malvern Hills.

On the way to Worcester we found a signpost to a Viewpoint so we thought we should investigate.

It was the Ketch Viewpoint.
It has a view of the Malvern Hills, the road intersections, and over the site of the Battlefields in the English civil war.

We were close to the river and followed a footpath sign to the Severn Way.

We missed the path and ended up on the roadside again. The driver had a little rant about the sign being misleading. I think he was feeling tired again.

We found the real path and went for a short walk alongside the Severn. We both agreed that it was not our favourite part of the river for walking, and we turned back to the car.

We drove through **Worcester** and admired the Railway Bridge by Foregate Street Station.

The bridge is a Grade II listed building, and it has 3 shields on the side.

Right hand side: A castle shield with the words 'FLOREAT SEMPER FIDELIS CIVITAS' which translate as 'Let the faithful city ever flourish' This is a reference to loyalty to the Royalist cause during the civil war.

Middle: The coat of arms of the Great Westen Railway.

Left hand side: A shield with three black pears and the words 'CIVITAS IN BELLO IN PACE FIDELIS' which translate as 'The city faithful in war and in peace'.

It is said that when Queen Elizabeth I saw a pear tree in Foregate on a visit in 1575 she asked that the pear be added to the city's coat of arms.

We parked by the Racecourse in Worcester and walked down to the river Severn which runs nearby.

There were rowing boats for hire and I was very torn. I wanted to take a boat out, but I really needed a loo stop, and a drink.

In the end the need for a comfort break won, and we decided to leave the boats for another day. We drove on towards **Droitwich Spa** looking for somewhere to stop, and found the **Copcut Elm** by the side of the A38. We took all our maps into the pub, and over a cup of coffee we held a planning meeting.

We found that there was a salt water Lido in Droitwich. It uses the salt from the brine streams flowing under the town which is built on substantial deposits of salt. So we drove there and found that it would not be open until later in the year. Disappointment.

Between Worcester and Birmingham the A38 follows the line of a Saxon salt road. The driver thought that we should check out the Brine Baths, but in the end we decided not to go in.

I didn't write down the reason for this, perhaps the opening times weren't right. It is a shame as the Brine Baths have since been closed, and we have missed the opportunity.

During our planning meeting we had decided to drive out on the roads to the east of the A38. We headed for **Hanbury Warf** on the Worcester and Birmingham canal. We had a look round the Chandlery. We looked at the prices of the canal boats, and realised that we couldn't afford one.

We watched the ducks and the jackdaws on the grass. And then – we saw a woodpecker. Another Greater Spotted Woodpecker. Around fifty years without seeing one woodpecker and then two seen in two days! We felt privileged.

Driving on we found Hanbury Church.

We stopped and walked through the footpaths around the church. The wild flowers were stunning, and we saw a fox coming up through the grass.

The church is built on top of a hill and there are panoramic views of the surrounding country.

There is a viewpoint marker with 'FROM THE PEOPLE OF HANBURY 2000' carved into the stone.

We appreciated this very much, thanks people of Hanbury. It told us that we could see the rivers Avon, Severn and Teme, that we had a view over Worcester, and that the hills we could see were the Cotswolds, Madams Hill, Bredon Hill and the Malvern Hills.

It is a very attractive marker. We thought that we would like to come back here and do some more walking one day.

Next we made a tour of the pubs in this area marked on our Ordinance Survey map to see if any of them did accomodation. We didn't find one, but we stopped at Lock 18 (Bridge 40) on the Worcester and Birmingham Canal, took some more pictures of ducks and bollards, and thought we would walk along the towpath to the next lock.

The driver took a picture of a small bird in the reeds. What is it?" he said.
"I don't know," I said.

At Lock 17 the driver took pictures of a train, a field of wheat...

...and me...

...while I took pictures of lichen.

Back at the car we looked at my Sat Nav for possible places to stay.

We asked at the Travel Inns, Travelodges, and Holiday Inn.

They were all fully booked. The people we spoke to said that there was a conference going on in Birmingham, and that the rooms had all been taken by people going to the event.

There was one other option shown on the Sat Nav. We phoned up and they had a room, so we booked it. Then we used the Sat Nav to drive to the hotel. We drove up the drive.

We were both thinking, "Wow!"

"Do you think they will let us in?" I said to the driver. "It looks a bit posh."

This was our first sight of the **Chateau Impney**. It looked like a fairy tale castle.

Of course, they let us in. It was just as impressive on the inside. Our room was called Eleonore and it had a view over the park and the helipad.

"A bit different from the Holiday Inn," said the driver.

We were too late to book a table in the restaurant in the Chateau so we went into Droitwich and found an italian restaurant called **Rossini**. It was very pleasant and the food was delicious, but it was fairly costly.

The service was a little slow, probably not a problem if you are out for a romantic evening, but we had been exploring all day and were very hungry by this time.

But – what a day!

Day 12

Wednesday 23rd May 2007

We woke up in the beautiful Chateau Impney.

There were postcards in the room with a picture of the Chateau. How lovely. I wrote a couple and took them to reception for posting. We were still sending a postcard a day up that remote track in Wales.

The A38 runs past the Chateau and it was an important transport route to the river Severn for salt from Droitwich Spa. Salt was also significant in the building of the Chateau.

The postcards have a brief history on the back:

Son of a wealthy bargee from Staffordshire, John Corbett pursued his ambition as an engineer and at the age of 28 bought up the derelict salt works at Stoke Prior. With his engineering skill his salt works became profitable, producing 160,000 tons per annum.

During his visit to Paris, Corbbett fell in love with a beautiful French governess whom he later married and as both had been enchanted by Versailles and the French chateaux decided to build one for themselves in England. This was Chateau Impney. Leading architects of today claim that the Chateau is unique and a brilliant example of design, artistry and elegance. If rebuilt today its cost would be in excess of 20 million pounds, and it will probably still be standing on a thousand years time due to its wonderful construction.

Three thousand men toiled on it, changing the landscape and creating lakes and waterfalls (for electricity), tropical gardens, beautiful golden décor and art work. In the Chateau's several hundred acres of parkland Corbett planted some 3,000 varieties of trees, many of which are today in their full magnificence and glory.

After breakfast we walked around the chateau grounds, the formal gardens and the fountains.

It was a warm sunny day, and the geese, ducks, sheep, cows, horses and squirrels all seemed to be as happy as we were.

The driver took some photographs of fish in the ponds. These were about as successful as his pictures of swallows had been.

We have been back to the chateau on a number of occasions, it is an amazing place. It had one problem – the coffee they served was awful. I understand that the hotel has changed hands recently; I hope that the new owners will keep all the charm that we loved, but improve the coffee.

Next, for the sake of completeness, we drove in a loop around Droitwich on the A38 and then took the road through the middle (B4090) which was the original road. Then we drove on up the A38. We saw a sign for the **Avoncroft Museum** and thought that this deserved a closer look.

The Museum turned out to be a collection of historic buildings. We were enchanted by this Co-op building, and the thought that buildings had been dismantled, brought to the museum and rebuilt.

We bought some lunch and ate it in the picnic area, before setting off to explore the buildings.

We wandered round barns and houses. There was a cell block, a cockpit and a house sized dovecot. "Wouldn't like to have been the person who had to clean that out," the driver said.

There was a windmill that you could turn to face the wind.

There was an ice house. Do you remember the ice house at Killerton House (Day 5)? The one at the museum looked very similar.

It was a fair walk round all the buildings and it was all very interesting. There was an ornately fitted showman's waggon. It was made in 1910 by Orton and Spooner in Burton on Trent and it belonged to the showman Tom Clarke. There was a description of the wagon on a board:

The Living Waggon cost Tom Clarke £1000. The exterior is clad in Spanish mahogany, and visitors may note that the window in the door carries the owner's name, decoratively etched into the glass.

What distinguishes the waggon from other surviving examples is the remarkable quality of its interior. The living room is sumptuously fitted with a ceiling bearing both carved and painted decoration. The painted putti on the ceiling, harking back to the art of the Italian Renaissance, was painstakingly applied. The mixture of flowers, richly coloured fruit and tiny landscape scenes would make the waggon exceptional in any circumstance. The fact that it survives in such remarkable condition makes it unique.

In practical terms the waggon was considerably sophisticated. It was delivered complete with an electric lighting system (the power being supplied by batteries), a remarkable innovation in an era still reliant on spirit lamps and gas lights even in permanent dwellings. A 'Hostess' stove set in an ornate chimneypiece, provided both warmth and a means of cooking. In the bedroom, a fitted washbasin conceals a safe.

We both also loved the prefab house, it was full of things we remembered from our childhoods.

"Look", I said to the driver, "Gloy glue."

We both agreed that we had forgotten it until we saw it there.

We looked at the telephone box collection.

I said, "Do you remember when you had to press button A and button B?"

We played at being Doctor Who's companions.

"It's bigger on the inside," I said.
"It isn't you know," the driver said.

There was a display about how bricks are made, and miniature bricks that you could buy for a pound. These were being sold to raise money for the museum. We bought one of the bricks in the gift shop, and today it sits on our dresser in the dining room as a reminder of our holiday.

Close to the entrance of the museum is a round building.

It is the counting house that used to stand in Bromsgrove Cattle Market. Inside the counting house we found Mr Roy Hawkesworth.

He told us about the building, and we told him about our trip.

We asked him if we could take a photograph of him, and he said yes. He suggested that we should go to Monument Lane in Lickey, as you could see views of Birmingham from there.

So that's what we did next. We found **Monument Lane** but it had a Road Closed sign on it. We parked and went to look at the monument. The monument had a plaque on it with gold lettering:

ERECTED
BY THE WORCESTERSHIRE REGIMENT OF YEOMANRY CAVALRY
TO MARK THEIR LASTING GRATITUDE
TO THE HONOURED MEMORY
OF THEIR BELOVED AND LAMENTED COLONEL COMMANDANT
AND BY THE COUNTY AT LARGE
TO COMMEMORATE
THE DISINTERESTED, SOLID AND EFFICIENT
PUBLIC SERVICES
AND
TO COMMEND TO IMITATION
THE EXEMPLARY PRIVATE VIRTUES
OF
OTHER ARCHER SIXTH EARL OF PLYMOUTH

"What 'Other' archer" we said, "Is it his name?" "Disinterested, solid and efficient, with exemplary private virtues," we said.

So I looked him up and found that his name was 'Other', he was born in the late 18th Century and was the Earl of Plymouth. Apparently the name comes from a Viking ancestor.

The driver took some photographs of the views from here and then we decided to drive round to the other end of Monument Lane. Here we found a **Lickey Hills Country Park** car park.

The park is magnificent, and has tremendous views. From the car park you could see over the countryside away from Birmingham. I would have liked to have walked around much more of it, but we had already ambled round the Chateau Impney grounds and the Avoncroft museum, as my knees were letting me know.

According to the map board in the car park we were on Beacon Hill. The board showed a '**Toposcope**'. "What is a Toposcope?" I said. We were not sure, so we set off to find it.

On the brow of the hill was a little castle. It had a metal circular map to show what you could see around you, and the views were amazing.

It was a shame that people had drawn on the map with felt tip.

What is a toposcope? We thought it might be the castle itself, a name for a viewing platform on top of a hill.

We were wrong. I looked it up and found that the word refers to the marker map which shows you what you can see from a high up point.

So we had already seen a toposcope the day before, at Hanbury church!

We both took many photographs of the views, and we were there ages using the map to find what we were seeing.

Thanks again Mr Hawkesworth, we would have missed this if you hadn't told us about it.

We knew that Stourbridge Crystal folk club met on a Wednesday night, and we thought we could see if we could find it.

We drove towards **Stourbridge**, and then with the aid of a street map we wove through the roads towards **The Bird in Hand** in Hagley Road. We wanted to make sure that we could get there without using another 'A road', so our route was not the most direct.

In fact it was quite tricky, but we made it to the end of the road and found that it was a 'No Entry' road.

We had difficulty finding the pub, so the driver phoned Anne Adams who runs the club. She told us that it was a small pub next to the glassworks. We found the pub, it had looked just like a white painted house from where we were sitting.

Having established where we were going for the evening, we looked for somewhere to stay.

The Sat Nav suggested the Innkeepers Lodge in Kingswinford. We booked a room, and drove there. The hotel rooms were in Summerhill House, a Georgian mansion built in 1756.

It was a comfortable room. The pub next door was a Harvester, and we had dinner there. Then we went back to Stourbridge to the folk club in the Bird in Hand, and spent a very pleasant evening.

I have looked for Summerhill House on the Innkeepers Lodge website, and I'm not sure it is currently a hotel.

The Crystal Folk Club is still run by Anne Adams, but has changed its name to the Crystal Music Club, is no longer at the Bird in Hand, and they now meet on a Friday evening.

Day 13

Thursday 24th May 2007

We had breakfast in the Harvester garden. We read the paper, and had more coffee. It was a very relaxing start to the day.

Next we drove back to Bromsgrove to pick up the A38 where we had left it. We drove to **Selly Oak** and parked in the station car park. There we found a striking pyramid with some words cut out in the metal. There were words around the top, around the middle and around the base of the pyramid.

The top line was:
Birmingham toys, all men praise, And riches spring daily from Birmingham toys.

The middle section said:
Not Europe can match us for traffic. America, Asia and Afric, Of what we invent each partakes of a share, For the best of wrought metals is Birmingham ware.

And around the base was:
Since by the canal navigation, of coals we've the best in the Nation, Around the circle your bumpers then put, For the cut of all cuts is the Birmingham cut. Birmingham cut, fairly wrought, For the cut of all cuts is a Birmingham cut.

From the internet I have found out that the words are taken from a song called **Birmingham Lads** written by John Freeth.

The tune he used was composed by Charles Dibden for the lyrics of 'The Warwickshire Lad'. I feel an affinity here as Charles Dibden was one of my ancestors. The song was written to mark the opening of the Birmingham Canal.

I found an interesting website called www.revolutionaryplayers.org.uk which has information about the history of the Industrial Revolution in the Midlands. The site has a digital library and in the section labelled 'Poems' is a book by John Freeth. The front page of the book shows:

INLAND NAVIGATION
AN
ODE.
HUMBLY INSCRIBED TO
The INHABITANTS of <i>Birmingham</i>,
AND
PROPRIETORS of the CANAL.
The SECOND EDITION.
By J.FREETH
BIRMINGHAM:
Printed for the AUTHOR, 1769.
[Price SIX – PENCE]

Pages 11 and 12 have the words of 'Birmingham Lads' and you can see that there are three differences between the words on the pyramid and the words printed in this book. The most obvious is that the book shows '*Around the gay circle your bumpers then put*' which improves the scan of the lyrics.

The station in Selly Oak is close to the Worcester and Birmingham Canal and we walked along the towpath towards Bournville. This stretch of the canal gave us a mixture of waterway, railway and city. We saw ducks and ducklings, Canada geese and goslings.

I know that some people dislike Canada geese, because they eat crops and make lots of mess where they live. We like them though. They were first brought to Britain in 1665 to live with the waterfowl collection of Charles II in St James Park.

There were yellow irises, red poppies and red hot pokers. There was grafitti (some of which we admired), barbed wire and rubbish.

There was a gate through to Selly Oak Hospital, but it was locked, so I don't think people could come out to the canal from there.

I took some more bollard pictures.

We could see the **Bournville** sign and the **Cadbury** factory. I put my camera through the fence so that I could take a picture without the wire of the fence.

The station at Bournville was painted in the Cadbury colours.

There were cut-out pictures in the metal work. It was very attractive, and it made me want to eat chocolate.

We caught the train back to Selly Oak.

Then we drove up the A38 into **Birmingham** and turned off into Holliday Street. We parked in the Central Square multi-story car park. From here we went to Warfside Street and down to the Canals. Apparently Birmingham has a more extensive canal waterway than Venice!

We walked along the Gas Street side of the canal. We looked at the Worcester Bar (it's not a pub) in the **Gas Street Basin**. The Bar was a 'canal-block' between the Worcester and Birmingham Canal and the Birmingham Canal as they were built by two different companies. The Birmingham Canal was built first and their company didn't want the other stealing their water.

There is a channel through between the canals now. We decided that the best way to see the canals was to take a boat tour, so we went on a leisurely trip on a boat called 'Dragonfly'

We took lots of pictures of bridges and boats, and had a thoroughly good time.

We took pictures of the canal signpost at the **Old Turn Junction**.

This signpost stands on a circular island, and Canada geese were making good use of it. Apparently the island wasn't put in for the signpost, as the island was built during the second World War and the post was added in 1983.

When we got off the Dragonfly we went to a pub called **The Malthouse**, which stands very near to the Old Turn Junction.

We had seen it from the boat and thought it would be a good place to sit in the sun and watch the canal traffic. It stands at the junction of three canals. We had a late lunch (3:30pm) of ham, egg and chips, and drank fizzy water and coffee.

We watched a grey, unpainted narrowboat go down the Worcester and Birmingham Canal. Sitting in the sun and relaxing, life was good.

We were both inspired enough to take pictures of the mirrors in the pub toilets…

…as we found out when we compared our photographs that evening. What does that say about us?

After lunch we went back to the car and drove through the tunnels to the Aston Express Way (where the A38 becomes a motorway for a while) and then took the **A5127** signposted to **Aston**. This was because the road follows the old route of the A38 and we felt it should be driven over.

We drove along the road to **Spagetti Junction**. If we it had been earlier in the day we would have liked to go to **Aston Hall**, so we put it on our 'to visit another day' list.

We parked at **Salford Park** near the five-a-side football pitches. We had often driven the M6 and A38(M) motorways, past here, and had glimpsed the water.

We had no idea that there was a park and such a big lake here.

We walked around the lake (which is also a resevoir), under the road to the river, and then to the canal. We saw geese and goslings, ducks and ducklings and a nesting swan.

There were dragonflies which the driver photographed. There were fishermen, lupins, and graffiti.

There are other junctions. The River Tame meets both the River Rea and the Hockley Brook. Three canals meet; the Grand Union Canal, the Birmingham and Fazeley Canal and the Tame Valley Canal

There are railway line junctions, gas pipelines and electric cables as well as some of the area's local roads.

We felt sure that there must be ley lines too.

There were some places which we found a little scary, but we will never again drive along the Aston Expressway without thinking of the park.

Next we went to see what **Star City** was, because we liked the name. We decided that it was probably not our thing. "It looks like an expensive place to bring teenage daughters," I said, and the driver just grunted.

Then we went to the Currys in **Ravenside Retail Park,** Erdington to buy some blank DVDs. We were running out of space on the laptop, so we needed to transfer some of our photographs to DVD.

At the Minworth Island roundabout we turned off the A38 and went down Lindridge Drive and then to Walmley Ash Lane. We needed to make a booking at the Travelodge at Barton under Needwood where we planned to stay two nights, so we were looking for somewhere quiet to park so that the driver could phone them.

We stopped outside the gate of the **Forge Farm Allotments**. The driver phoned the Travelodge (This is the Travelodge Burton A38 Northbound). They said that they had a room for two nights, but asked the driver to phone the Central Bookings number to make the booking.

The driver phoned the Central Bookings number, and got very cross with the automated booking service. He was speaking carefully and clearly (but slightly crossly) into the phone.

I decided to get out of the car and look through the gate at the allotments. There were blackbirds and sparrows hunting on the ground.

The driver ran out of credit on his phone just before he completed the booking process. More huffiness.

He phoned for credit, and then phoned the Central Bookings number again, and spoke carefully and clearly (but more crossly) to the robot at the other end of the phone.

I saw a pair of lapwings in the allotments, and would have liked to have pointed them out to the driver, but he was busy, speaking carefully. I didn't get a picture of the lapwings (they flew away), but I did get a picture of an irate driver.

We drove on. The driver told me what he thought of automated booking systems, and I told him about the lapwings. We drove along Wiggins Hill Road towards the canal, and stopped to take a picture of Birmingham (from the other direction from the Lickey Hills).

We saw a barn which was very similar to one we had seen at the Avoncroft museum. "That barn looks very like one we saw at the Avoncroft museum," I said and the driver grunted. He was still thinking about the robot booking system.

We found the Wiggins Hill Bridge over the **Birmingham and Fazeley Canal**. At the side of the canal we found the **Kingsley Canalside** pub. We bought two pints and took them out to the bench by the canal to watch the sun going down.

While we were sitting there, we saw the same grey boat that we had seen in the centre of Birmingham earlier in the day! It came past us and moored.

We had a chat with the people on the boat and they said that they had come through 27 locks to get there.

They must have been very ready for a pint in the pub.

We talked about kayaking and they told us that the stretch between Fradley Junction and Huddlesford on the Coventy canal was a good one as there were no locks.

We have since canoed this stretch and picnicked at Fradley Junction. Thanks again for the advice – very useful.

We watched the sun go down, and sat in the dusk, drinking our beer and watching bats fly past us.

Next we drove back to the Minworth Roundabout, so that we could go to the enormous Asda we had passed earlier. We bought some supplies for supper, and then drove up the A38 to the Travelodge.

We had supper in bed while we watched some more episodes of Survivors.

Day 14

Friday 25th May 2007

We watched the last episode of Survivors in Series 1 in our Travelodge room. Then we had breakfast in the **Little Chef** next door.

The driver had an Olympian breakfast and I had a more modest selection.

We both spent a while taking photographs of traffic on the A38 from the window. We were trying to capture a picture of speed, and to have traffic on both sides of the carriageway. Most of the pictures show empty road where a car or lorry has just been.

When we went to pay we bought some maps and then realised that we hadn't claimed our 25% discount on the breakfast. We were due this because we had stayed at the Travelodge. Apparently it was too late to make the claim, and we both felt a little aggreived.

I like Little Chef, and would often seek it out when I was working away from home. I like the fish and chips, and the pancakes. The Little Chef next to the Northbound Burton Travelodge is closed now, and the building is shuttered up. It looks a bit sad, and must make life awkward for people wanting to stay in the hotel.

We drove back down the A38 past Lichfield to visit the **Heart of the Country Craft Centre**. We had passed this often before, and I was interested to see what it was like. It turned out to be a shopping village with some interesting shops and restaurants.

In the car park there was a very small bridge, and we wondered what it was for.

Outside one of the shops there was a nesting blackbird, which we tried hard to look at without disturbing it. The driver took a picture, but the bird was quite well camouflaged. We know what it is, but it wouldn't mean much to you.

In the courtyard there was a fountain made using a milk churn. It was very attactive and it set the driver reminiscing about when he was young and they had a house cow, and there was always too much milk.

We were far too full of breakfast to sample anything in the restaurants, but we had a look round the shops. I was very taken with a bronze hare, but it was more money than we could afford. I took a picture of it though.

"Look," I said to the driver, "I have done some virtual shopping."
"It could catch on," he said, "much better than cluttering up the house with things." I still would have liked the hare though.

Next we thought we would go and look at the **Coventry Canal**, and the place suggested by the people in the grey boat the evening before. We drove towards Huddlesford and parked opposite a pub called **The Plough** in Huddlesford Lane.

We went on to the canal towpath and under bridge 83. There was some work being done on the railway bridge near to the Plough, so we walked the other way towards Streethay Warf. We remarked on the rich collection of flowers and grasses along the way. We found a patch of vine-like plants with white flowers.

"What's that?" said the driver.
"I don't know," I said. He took a picture so that I could identify it later.

It was white byony. I thought it was very pretty, but apparently it is invasive, poisonous and destructive.

We walked past a pair of white ducks swimming and then through Streethay Wharf. I took some pictures of bollards.

Just past the wharf the canal runs parallel to the A38. We walked on to Streethay Bridge (Bridge 86). This is a little bridge with grass growing on it.

The driver took twenty one pictures of me while traffic went past. You can put them together to make a little video of lorries and cars speeding past a woman sitting on a canal bridge.

I took one picture of the driver photographing the canal and the road at the same time. By this time we had become very fond of the A38, and felt that it was 'our road'. It was a noisy place to sit, but we liked it.

We walked back to the car and drove to **Fradley Junction** which is where the Coventry Canal finishes.

There was a British Waterways information board at the junction:

Welcome to Fradley Junction, the meeting place of the Coventry and Trent & Mersey Canals.

The junction was built in the 1780s by the Coventry Canal Company and the Trent and Mersey Canal Company. The brick buildings you can see here were once a toll-house, forge, carpentry workshop and stables. They have now been renovated as visitor facilities, offices and residential accomodation.

We bought some lunch in the café and sat in the gravelled courtyard area outside the shop, watching the chaffinches and the boats.

There was a British Waterways Ford van in the courtyard, and the driver took pictures of the exterior and interior, and reminisced about when he was a boy.

On the other side of the **Trent and Mersey Canal** there is a nature reserve. The British Waterways board has this information about the reserve:

Water Feuds

Fradley Resevoir lies just over the canal and was part of a historic water feud between the two canal companies.

Water is vital to any canal and the Trent & Mersey Canal Company did not want to loose any of theirs to the Coventry Canal. In the 1780s they dug Fradley resevoir to store overflow water from the Trent & Mersey Canal. When needed this was diverted back into their canal with not a drop being lost to their rival canal.

The reserve was a very lovely place. It had lots of carved wooden sculptures, carved benches and there were dipping platforms made out of recycled plastic. We were impressed by these, they weren't slippery, and they held the heat from the sun so they felt warm to sit on.

We walked around the pool, watched a common tern wheeling and diving, hand fed some tame goslings, and saw coots, white ducks and yellow ducklings, and squirrels.

There were some places which were spread all soft with willow down.

There was a wooden hide, decorated with wooden and painted reed mace (I would call these bullrushes, as would most people, but I know that some purists are upset by this).

The inside of the hide reminded us of the Bear Hut at Killerton (Day 5). We spent some time watching blue tits from the hide.

Next we walked up the the wharf past the Swan Inn. We didn't go into the Swan, but we have been back since, both by car and by kayak, and they do a very good pint of Black Sheep bitter in there. They also have a folk meeting on Thursday nights.

Wikipedia has an entry about Fradley Junction which tells you that it is popular with gongoozlers.

'Gongoozler' – well I needed to look that one up!

Apparently this is someone who likes to watch boats and other things on and around canals.

We had been gongoozling, and hadn't realised it!

Next we drove on up the A38.

The road became very busy so we turned off to go to **Alrewas**. We parked and walked down a path and discovered another beautiful place where rivers and canal meet.

We walked along the canal and took a few photographs of a multi-coloured duckling family.

The village has several pubs and we looked at the George and Dragon and the Crown. In the end we settled on the George and Dragon and had supper there:
Driver: Trio of lamb chops
Me: Duck (was this appopriate?)

It was all very good. We have been back to Alrewas a number of times and can also recommend the Crown. Have a look at the mosaics and paintings in the car park if you visit.

Afterwards we drove out to **Blithfield Resevoir**. We were attracted by the map as it showed that there was a road across the middle of the resevoir.

We watched the sun set, and both took lots of pictures of the sun going down over the water.

We knew that the **Brewtown Folk Club** met at the **Star and Garter** in Burton on a Friday night, so we went there. No folk club – the person behind the bar told us that the club was closed for the summer.

This was a shame but we had a pint in the pub and then went back to the Travelodge on the A38. It had already been another crowded day.

The Brewtown Club now meets at the **Old Cottage Tavern**, probably best to check it out first.

Day 15

Saturday 26th May 2007

From our room at the Travelodge we could see boats passing along the Trent and Mersey Canal. We could also see the Marina on the other side of the canal.

We decided not to breakfast at the Little Chef, but packed up the car and left it in the Travelodge car park. We walked along the canal towpath towards **Branston Water Park**.

This is a very noisy stretch of the Trent and Mersey Canal. There are industrial activities on one side and the A38 running parallel on the other side. There were compensations. The towpath flowers were blooming, there were ducklings, and the weather was fine.

We took pictures of red clover, yellow hawkweed, blue alkanet, and plantain clumps. We fired plantain missiles at each other.

We passed a field. "Are those llamas?" I said.

"They look like llama," the driver said, and took some more pictures.

I have looked it up and there is a place off the A38 where you can go trekking with a llama, and have a picnic in a yurt. If you want to look it up you can search for **National Forest Llama Treks**.

The canal goes through Branston Water Park which was created from flooded gravel pits. There are paths off from the canal to the park. There are islands and reed beds, water birds, and walks around the park.

The driver had another attempt at photographing a fish, and then turned his attention to the swallows. We have some photographs of an image in the water, and you can definitely see that it is a fish.

There are a lot more photographs of blurry swallows (remember Day 3 on Dartmoor and Day 10 by the Red Lion and Lower Lode Lane?). The pictures were getting better though.

This was Day 15 – and my knees were beginning to let me know that I had been over-doing the walking. We looked at the map and decided to separate.

I would walk on to **The Bridge Inn**, where I would sit and wait for the driver. The driver would walk back to the car and meet me at the Bridge.

The Bridge Inn turned out to be a good place to wait, and I had a cup of coffee. When the driver arrived we decided to have brunch. The pub is an Italian restaurant, so we both opted for pizza.
Driver: Milanese pizza
Me: Marinara pizza

After lunch we drove back down the A38 to visit the **Barton Turns Marina** – this was the marina we could see from our Travelodge window. We had a look at the shop and the boats, the ducks and the signs. There has been a lot more building at the marina since we visited in 2007. There are pubs and cafés and shops now.

Then we travelled back up the A38 towards Derby and past **Burton upon Trent**.

Burton is a brewing centre and there is more than one brewery in the town. If I had been up to the walking we would have visited the **Bass Brewing Museum.** We had both been recently, so decided to give it a miss this time. It is now called the National Brewery Centre.

"They make Marmite in Burton, as well as beer," the driver said.
"And Branston Pickle in Branston," I said.
"They used to", he said, "but I think it is made somewhere else now."

Our next stop was **Markeaton Park** just south of Derby. The park has a lake where you can take out a boat or pedalo, a brook and bridge where you can feed the ducks, a craft village where you can also buy duck food, a superb childrens play area, a boating lake for model boats, tennis courts and pitches. It even has its own railway with stations.

The driver had taken pictures of a number of railway lines over the last 15 days. He lay on the track to get this one. Not recommended, but it does include a view of the bridge over the A38.

It is a stunning footbridge with wide circular sweeps at either end and is a fine place to watch the star of the show – the A38.

On the other side from the park, the footbridge circles an impressive weeping willow.

From the bridge spiral you can see the ponds which are more parts of the Markeaton Brook. When you get down to ground level they are behind fences. We watched a mother moorhen feeding her chick. The fences probably protected her and the chick.

We walked a little way along this path as it was marked as part of the **Bonnie Prince Charlie Walk**. It wasn't the most interesting part of the walk, so we turned back to the car.

Apparently it is a waymarked route from Ashbourne to Derby and it follows the general direction of Prince Charles Edward Stuart's march in 1745.

In the car park the driver took 26 photographs of a squirrel raiding a litter bin. "You wouldn't do that with the old film cameras," he said.

When you view them quickly you get a flip book impression.

Next we turned off the A38 onto Kedlestone Road and took the Broadway to **Darley Abbey**.

The area gets its name from a monastry founded in the 12th Century, but destroyed in the 16th Century. It is now part of the Derwent Valley Mills heritage area, because of the mill and workers cottages built in the 18th Century by Thomas Evans.

The **Abbey** pub is one of the original buidings from the monastic era. We have been in the pub many times and can recommend it. It has lots of atmosphere and good beer.

We parked in the car park opposite the pub, and went to have a look at the **River Derwent**. We walked over the toll bridge road and then back again.

We watched a cricket match on the Darley Abbey cricket ground for a few minutes. Then we decided to go back towards the A38, drive the other direction along Keddleston Road and look for the **River Ecclesbourne.**

I haven't recorded whether we found the river. We did drive the B5023 past the **Puss In Boots** pub because I took a photograph of it (and the road signs).

Our next destination was **Keddleston Hall**.

"It's an impressive building," said the driver. "We must come back when it is open."

"Would you like to walk in the grounds?" he said.

I told him that I would very much like to walk in the grounds, but that my knees had other plans.

We have since been back and spent a day in the house and the grounds. It is a lovely place.

"What I would like is a cup of tea," I said. So we drove back to the A38 and up to **Little Eaton** to the Little Chef just off the A38.

The building now houses a Starbucks.

It was one of my favourite Little Chefs. If we didn't feel like cooking after work, we used to go there for our tea. Not often enough to keep it open it seems!

It was raining and the little Chef was cosy. We had a cup of tea, watched the traffic on the roundabout and bought a map.

There was no problem about where we would sleep that night. We were only five miles from home.

If you have a foolish desire to re-create the journey we made, then send me an email on

marianne.hulse@googlemail.com

and I will recommend somewhere to stay in **Belper**.

So home to the next episode of Doctor Who and our own bed. Tomorrow would see the end of the road.

Day 16

Sunday 27th May 2007

We awoke to a grey day and very heavy rain. It was similar to Day 2, except that from our house we didn't have decking and views over the sea. We could see the cemetery from the bedroom window, and it has some quite interesting trees.

After breakfast we drove back to Little Eaton to pick up the A38 again. It was such a miserable day that we decided to drive the A38 from Little Eaton to **Mansfield** without stopping along the way. We listened to the Archers Omnibus on the way.

11:35
We arrived at the end of the A38.

We felt that there should have been fanfares and fireworks. It was a grey miserable day and people were going about their own lives and took no notice of us. There was a café at the end of the road and we thought we would have a cup of coffee to celebrate - but it was closed.

We took some pictures of the end of the A38. This is called Stockwell Gate and there was a signpost showing the name.

We had a look for another place to get a coffee, but then decided to go somewhere else.

"Well, that's it then," the driver said.
"Perhaps we can find some interesting things on the way back," I said. "I don't really feel that we have done justice to Mansfield."

We drove back down the A38 and took a left turn down **Sheepbridge Lane**. Then we turned down **Bleak Hill Lane**. We could see that there were some ponds marked on the map.

What we found was a fence and beyond the fence a sign that said:

LITTLE BLEAKHILLS FISHERY
AND BIRD SANCTUARY

We rather liked the 'Bird Sanctury' bit and fished out our umbrellas to take a closer look.

Through the wire we could see some moorhens and a heron standing by the pond. The driver took pictures of the heron; the heron obliged by taking a flight around the pond and then came back to the same spot.

While the driver was occupied with the heron I walked a short way down the road and found a footpath and a way sign. We had found the **Oakham Local Nature Reserve**

We walked along the path through the Reserve and found a wildflower meadow which was probably the most full of different grasses and flowers that either of us had ever seen.

There were yellow hawkweed, white campion, egg and bacon plants, silverweed, clovers, vetch, forget-me-nots and speedwell, and these were just the plants I could name. It was very lovely.

We found a bank with holes in it.

"Kingfishers!" we said, and watched for a while.

Do you remember Day 9 at Slimbridge? We watched for kingfishers from a hide. And Day 10? We watched holes in a bank. It would have been so good to have seen a kingfisher on Day 16, the last day, but we didn't see anything.

I have since found that we may have been breaking the law by watching these holes. Under the Wildlife and Countryside Act 1981 kingfishers are designated Schedule 1 birds and they and their young must not be disturbed at the nest. Just by watching the holes, we may have disturbed the birds. I hope that we did not, it was certainly not our intention.

We followed the path and it went into a zig-zag above a pond, and then to a road (Hamilton Way). We crossed over the road, turned left and found the path on the other side. The path went over a bridge, along a board walk and followed the **River Maun**.

We turned back because my knees were painful. It was a struggle to walk the return journey.

We drove to the **Kingsmill Reservoir** (If we had carried on walking the path, this is where we would have ended up).

It was still raining, but we got the umbrellas out again. Around the side of the reservoir there were some pollarded willows. We remarked on how life strives so hard to survive.

Over the water there were lots of swallows. It reminded us of the line, 'Thick flies the skimming swallow', from the Robert Burns poem 'Composed in August.'

The driver took 35 photographs of skimming swallows, and I took 28.

Most of them show several blurred shapes over grey water. However, being there, and watching the birds was quite thrilling.

Previous swallow photography attempts were:

Day 3 Dartmoor
Day 10 River Severn
Day 15 Branston Water Park.

Our next stop was **Crich Tramway Village**. We drove the B roads to **Pentrich** and across **Wingfield Park** to **Crich**. There were magnificent views over the Amber Valley.

We were planning to spend the afternoon at the Tramway Village because the driver had been asked if he would like to play guitar and sing in the 'Folk on the Trams' event.

Here were more re-created buildings and old cars! Remember the Avoncroft Museum on Day 12? And the old cars outside the South Devon Railway (Day 3) and the British Waterways van at Fradley Junction (Day 14)? This had the added excitement of being able to ride on the trams.

And, if you had been there that day, you could have travelled on a tram in which the Driver was playing his guitar and singing. I'm not sure if that would have added to your enjoyment of the adventure.

One of the reconstructed buildings is a pub. There was singing and playing in there as well. It was a welcome place to sit out of the rain and enjoy a pint of beer.

The Tramway Museum also has a police box (Or is it a Tardis?) and it has some bollards.

From the car park at the Tramway Museum you can see the **Crich Stand**. It looks a bit like a light house, and you can see it from many places in Derbyshire. It is a war memorial for the Sherwood Foresters regiment. You can visit the tower on some days and climb the steps to the top. You are supposed to be able to see across eight counties from the top of the tower.

Next we went back to **Belper**. We went for a final diner in the **New Ming Court** restaurant.

We had:
Sesame prawn toast
Spare ribs
Crispy duck
Roast duck cantonese style
Egg fried rice
Prawns with oyster sauce
Beef with mushrooms.
An excellent feast to finish our journey.

(For anyone checking, you can't drive from Crich to the New Ming Court without using another A road, you have to travel the A609 for a short distance. But shouldn't you be doing something more interesting?)

We had a tremendously good holiday.

If you have joined us by reading this account, you have been very welcome.

Where did we go?

Day 0
Jamaica Inn, Westbury Hotel – Bodmin, The Barley Sheaf – Bodmin, The Hole in the Wall – Bodmin.

Day 1
Bodmin, The Start of the A38, Bridge over the River Fowey, Largin Wood, Trago Mills – Liskeard, Two Waters Foot, Carnglaze Caverns, Menheniot Station, Castle Air, River Seaton, Trerulefoot, Hessenford, Seaton, Portwrinkle, Finnygook Inn – Crafthole.

Day 2
Crafthole, Downderry, River Seaton, Bonyalva, Notter Bridge, River Lynher, Saltash Station, Mary Newman's Cottage, Tamar Bridge, Plymouth, Royal Albert Bridge, Bodmin, Plymouth, Buckfastleigh, Church House Inn – Rattery.

Day 3
Buckfast Butterflies and Dartmoor Otter Sanctuary, South Devon Steam Railway, River Dart, Dartmoor, Badgers Holt – Dartmeet, Burrator Reservoir, Sheepstor, Plympton, River Avon (Devon), Coombe Cross Hotel – Bovey Tracey.

Day 4
Chudleigh Knighton, Inchcape Garage – Exeter, Seven Stars – Exeter, River Exe, Exeter Ship Canal, Exeter City Walls, Topsham Lido, Topsham Quay, The Goat Walk, River Clyst, Broadclyst, The Red Lion – Broadclyst.

Day 5
Killerton House, Bickleigh Mill – Tiverton, River Exe, Devon Railway Centre and Model World, Sampford Peverell, Grand Western Canal Country Park, Halburton, Sampford Arundel, The Red Lion – Broadclyst.

Day 6
The Wellington Monument, Bathpool, Bridgewater and Taunton Canal, Somerset Space Walk, River Tone, Obridge Viaduct, The Children's Wood, Firepool, Maunsel Lock, Weston-super-Mare, Hutton Moor Leisure Centre, Weston-Super-Mare East Premier Inn.

Day 7
St Georges Garage – Weston-Super-Mare, Grand Pier – Weston, Birnbeck Pier – Weston, Claremont Wine Vaults – Weston, Cheddar Gorge, Clifton Suspension Bridge, River Avon (Bristol), Old Passage Inn – Arlingham.

Day 8
Bristol Harbour, The Cross Hands of Alveston, Thornbury Castle, Littleton on Severn, Oldbury on Severn, Whale Warf, Bristol's Time Gap, Old Passage Inn – Arlingham.

Day 9
Sharpness Docks, Slimbridge, Gloucester and Sharpness Canal, The Pilot Inn – Hardwicke, Gloucester Docks, Twigworth Premier Inn.

Day 10
The Red Lion – Norton, River Severn, Coombe Hill Nature Reserve, Lower Lode Lane, Tewkesbury, The Bell Hotel – Tewkesbury.

Day 11
Tewkesbury, River Avon (Warwickshire), Fleet Inn – Twyning, Ketch Viewpoint – Worcester, Worcester, Worcester Racecourse, River Severn, The Copcut Elm, Droitwich, Hanbury Warf, Worcester and Birmingham Canal, Hanbury Church, Chateau Impney, Rossini – Droitwich.

Day 12
Chateau Impney, Avoncroft Museum, Monument Lane – Lickey, Lickey Hills Country Park, Innkeepers Lodge – Kingswinford, Bird in Hand – Stourbridge.

Day 13
Selly Oak, Worcester and Birmingham Canal, Bournville Station, Selly Oak, Birmingham Canals, Gas Street Basin, The Malthouse – Old Turn Junction,Spagetti Junction, Salford Park, Aston Reservoir, Forge Farm Allotments, Kingsley Canalside, Birmingham and Fazeley Canal, Travelodge Burton A38 Northbound.

Day 14
Heart of the Country Craft Centre, Coventry Canal, Fradley Junction,Trent and Mersey CanalAlrewas, George and Dragon – Alrewas, Blithfield Resevoir, Star and Garter – Burton, Travelodge Burton A38 Northbound.

Day 15
Trent and Mersey Canal, Branston Water Park, The Bridge Inn – Branston, Barton Turns Marina, Markeaton Park, Bonnie Prince Charlie Walk, Darley Abbey, River Derwent, Keddleston Hall, Little Eaton.

Day 16
Little Eaton, Mansfield, The End of the A38, Little Bleakhills Fishery and Bird Sanctury, Oakham Local Nature Reserve, River Maun, Kingsmill Reservoir, Crich Tramway Village, New Ming Court, Belper.

Some costs

Some amounts that I recorded, and some that I know I missed. There are lots of others that I didn't write down, so I can't tell you the overall cost.

Food and Drink

Day 0
Strensham Services — £12.04
Jamaica Inn — £24.00

Day 1
Trago Mills £1.40
Seaton Beach Café — £13.55
Finneygook Inn — £8.40

Day 2
Notter Bridge Riverside Inn — £3.30
Plymouth Station — £5.28
Church House Inn Rattery — £31.60

Day 3
Badgers Holt — £03.20
Sainsburys — £21.20

Day 4
Seven Stars Exeter — £12.25
Red Lion, Broadclyst — £52.50

Day 5
Devon Railway Centre — ?
Red Lion, Broadclyst — £43.15

Day 6
Maunsel Lock — £6.00
Pavillion Beefeater, Hutton Moor — £16.66

Day 7
Old Passage Inn — £48.70

Day 8
Bristol Docks ice cream — £4.00
Bristol Docks bacon sandwich — £6.50

Day 9
Slimbridge — £8.90
Pilot Inn — £26.40

Day 10
Red Lion Inn Gloucester — £27.52
Bell Hotel — £32.50

Day 11
Rossini Droitwich   £69.15

Day 12
Avoncroft Museum   ?
Harvester Stourbridge   ?

Day 13
The Malthouse   ?

Day 14
Little Chef, Barton   £15.72
Fradley Junction   £11.23

Day 15
The Bridge Inn   £15.20
Little Chef, Little Eaton   £3.38

Day 16
Ming Court   £32.00

Accomodation

Day 0
Westbury Hotel   £68.00

Day 1
B&B by the Sea   £55.00

Day 2
Kilbury Manor Farm   £70.00

Day 3
Coombe Cross Hotel   £90.00

Days 4 and 5
Red Lion Broadclyst   £104.00

Day 6
Premier Travel Inn Weston   £55.00

Days 7 and 8
Old Passage Inn   £220.00

Day 9
Premier Travel Inn Twigworth   £48.00

Day 10
Bell Hotel Tewkesbury   £65.00

Day 11
Chateau Impney   £79.90

Day 12
Innkeepers Lodge   £52.50

Days 13 and 14
Travelodge   ?

Days 15 and 16
Home..   00.00

Petrol

Day 0
Strensham Services   £30.04

Day 1
Shell Caradon, Trerulefoot   £40.50

Day 3
Shell Carew A38 South Brent   £15.01
Oil   £9.99

Day 7
Southvill Bristol   £37.51

Day 12
Swan Bromsgrove   £36.10

Other

Day 0
Services, Maps   £29.55

Day 1
Millets, Mugs   £3.98
WH Smith, Plastic Wallets   £1.94

Day 2
Taymar Toll Bridge   £1.00
Plymouth Station Car Park   £2.00
Plymouth to Bodmin Return   £12.00

Day 3
Otters and Butterflies   £13.00
Otters and Butterflies Gift Shop £22.90
Badgers Holt Biscuits   £12.06

Day 4
Exeter Car Park   £1.50
Topsham Swimming Pool   £5.00

Day 5
Killerton ?	
Killerton Gift shop	£9.08
Devon Railway Centre	£11.20

Day 6
Maunsel Lock, Tin Mugs	£9.00
Asda £14.75	
Weston Leisure Centre	£6.50

Day 7
Weston Pier Train	80p
Weston Postcards/Paper	£2.57
St Georges Garage	£130.02
Riverside Inn Cheddar Car Park	£3.00

Day 8
Bristol Docks Car Park	£2.60
Bristol Docks Boat Trip	£9.00
Wapping Warf Car Park	£2.60

Day 9
Slimbridge	£12.30

Day 11
Tewkesbury Boat Trip	£12.00
Red Cross T shirts	£5.74

Day 12
Avoncroft Museum	£13.00
Avoncroft Museum brick	£1.00

Day 13
Train – Bournville to Selly Oak	£2.80
Birmingham Boat Trip	£6.00

Day 14
Little Chef, Maps	£24.97
Fradley Car Park	£1.00

Day 16
Little Chef, Map	£3.75

Postscript

This is an account of our journey. There must be hundreds of places along the way that we didn't stop or visit which were just as good as the ones we found.

Two people can only do so much in sixteen days. You should go out and discover the other places for yourself.

Is there anything we would have done differently? We should have designed in some rest days and taken a longer time. We needed a holiday to get over this one.

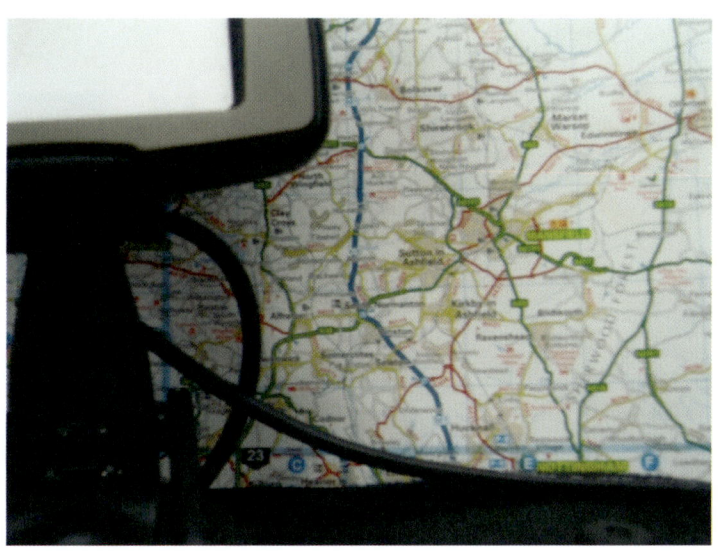

Printed in Great Britain
by Amazon